THE MAN WHO WOULD NOT DIE

Fifty Years Afterwards.

The Man Who Would Not Die

by

**Desmond L. Plunkett &
The Reverend R. Pletts**

The Pentland Press Limited
Edinburgh · Cambridge · Durham · USA

First published in 2000 by
The Pentland Press Ltd.
1 Hutton Close
South Church
Bishop Auckland
Durham

British Library Cataloguing in Publication Data.
A catalogue record for this book is available
from the British Library.

ISBN 1 85821 726 1

Typeset by George Wishart & Associates, Whitley Bay.
Printed and bound by Antony Rowe Ltd., Chippenham.

This book is dedicated to all those who are or have been prisoners, whether physical, spiritual, mental or emotional.

One hour of life, crowded to the full with glorious
action, and filled with noble risks, is worth whole
years of mean observances of paltry decorum.

Walter Scott

High Flight

Oh! I have slipped the surly bonds of Earth
And danced the skies on laughter-silvered wings;
Sunward I've climbed and joined the tumbling mirth
Of sun-split clouds – and done a hundred things
You have not dreamed of – wheeled and soared and swung
High in the sun-lit silence. Hov'ring there
I've chased the shouting wind along and flung
My eager craft through footless halls of air,
Up, up the long delirious burning blue.
I've topped the wind-swept heights with easy grace
Where never lark nor eagle flew;
And, while with silent, lifting mind I've trod
The high untrespassed sanctity of space,
Put out my hand and touched the face of God.

*Written by Pilot Officer John Gillespie Magee, Jr. 1922-1941,
of 142 Squadron of the Royal Canadian Air Force, killed in
action over England, 11th December 1941, aged 19 years.*

Let Us Salute Them

Contents

Illustrations

Foreword

During the first two and a half years of the Second World War Britain relied very heavily upon its Air Force and many British and Allied airmen were shot down and captured. They were held as POWs in various prison camps which filled up rapidly.

Reichmarschall Hermann Goering was in overall charge of the Luftwaffe (German Air Force) and also of all Air Force prisoners. He decided that a special 'escape proof' camp should be constructed to house many of them. It was erected in a thick pine forest near Sagan in Silesia, in Germany, and was heavily guarded. It became the centre of the most dramatic and well known mass breakout of POWs during the war

Des Plunkett's life must rank as one of the most enthralling action-packed adventure stories. His great love of flying made him an instructor in the British Royal Air Force and later took him into enemy territory over Europe during the Second World War. After being shot down, he was a prisoner of war for three years and escaped death by the strangest circumstances on several occasions. He survived great odds. After the war his flying career continued in the Royal Air Force. Later, as a pilot and air surveyor, he saw vast areas of the Middle East, India, Asia and Africa. His escapes from death gave him a zest for life rarely seen in most people. He was a planner and participator in the famous tunnel escape from the German POW camp at Sagan, Stalag Luft III, which became known as 'The Great Escape'. Des was one who got away, only to be recaptured almost within reach of freedom. Imprisoned by the Gestapo he faced certain death but survived. Fifty of his colleagues were killed on capture. Des is one of the few surviving members of the Great Escape and this account recalls this incredible story. It is the story of one man's search for life which took him through some of the greatest events of this century, brought him into contact with many notable personalities and ultimately led him into the greatest freedom of all. It is a story of outstanding courage and some amazing luck – or was it more like divine intervention?

This is his story, and that of those who shared those dramatic times.

They were men of valour.

Fifty Years Afterwards

The date was March 1994, the place, Zagan (Sagan), Poland. Wrapped up against the cold a group of people were gathered in a small wood and watched a Polish military contingent smartly come to attention and lift their weapons skyward. The leading officers saluted and a volley of shots rang out. As the sound echoed away, silence settled upon the group. Their thoughts were filled with poignant memories. Moist eyes disclosed deep emotions. They were united by a common bond.

The Memorial to the fifty airmen who lost their lives.

*Survivors and friends 1994, and the remains of
the 'cooler' at Sagan. Des at left of hole talking to
Ivo Tonder; Sydney Douse back left.*

Long-lost loved ones, separated by empty years, seemed to draw
near and linger unseen. Seven elderly men stood together lost in
thought as they recalled the events which fifty years ago had
united them and now brought them back to the place where it
had all begun. It was from this very spot that seventy six men
including themselves had made a bid for freedom. Little now

remained of the prisoner of war camp that once stood there, just a trench and a few bricks.

These seven survivors, together with other families, friends and official representatives, had gathered in memory of 'the Fifty' who gave their lives during March and April of 1944 in their bid to escape from Stalag Luft III, Prisoner of War Camp in Sagan, Poland.

Amongst them stood a little man. The wind touched his thin, sandy coloured hair as he gazed at the proceedings, a twinkle in his eyes and a look of impish delight on his face. His stooped form and wrinkled face testified to his advanced age but despite his years he looked like a schoolboy enjoying a special outing. He carried a wealth of life's experiences and a clarity of memory for a time most others had forgotten and others never knew. He was a man who had lived through and witnessed terrible events and, while so many fell around him, he simply would not die.

As memories flooded over him his eyes misted, the gathering of people around him faded and his mind carried him to the past to recall the most incredible of all escapes.

CHAPTER 1

Through the Gates of Hell

The prisoner was about five foot eight inches tall and was dressed in shabby, weather-worn clothes. Because he was hunched with fatigue he looked small. He stood to one side of a large room, with his face about six inches away from the wall upon which he gazed intently. About twenty other prisoners stood or sat in silence, staring straight forward without ever moving their eyes.

They looked haggard. A sense of fear pervaded through the room. The hunched man was tired but there was still a twinkle in his eye. The two guards who stood at his side were dressed in black uniforms with scarlet trimmings and they looked smart but frightening. This was the standard uniform for all Czech gendarmes. The prisoner sneaked a glance at the other occupants of the room and this brought an immediate response from the guards.

'Keep your eyes on the wall!' they shouted.

Silence followed.

The prisoner sneaked another glance.

'Stop looking around!' came the command.

Again silence.

Once more the captive's eyes wandered.

'Stop it, stop it!' shouted the guards.

The prisoner seemed to enjoy baiting them and it also created some interest among the other captives. Who could this be who would tempt the wrath of the Gestapo?

1

The door opened and a tall Gestapo officer strode in. With a yell of anger he swung his heavy hand up and grabbed the prisoner by the back of the neck and smashed his head against the wall several times. The prisoner reeled under the force of the attack and clutched at the wall for support but it seemed to swim in front of him. His legs wobbled and he nearly passed out but, summoning his reserves, he straightened up.

'Stand up, stand up,' the officer yelled, 'Put your nose on the wall and do not move.'

The prisoner did so and found he could no longer focus his eyes which began to close.

'Keep your eyes open,' came the command and the prisoner jerked upright in fear of another head smashing.

The officer went out but after a while returned with a rush and a shout.

'March, March!' he yelled and with a powerful hand propelled the prisoner staggering down the passage to the door of a cell through which he was flung. The heavy door clanked shut and the sound of footsteps departed, leaving the prisoner with a sense of abandonment. Silence – he was alone to contemplate his fate.

How on earth had he landed in this mess, he wondered? Random thoughts filtered through his mind but he was too tired to gather them into any kind of logical order. He knew he was in serious trouble and would soon very likely get a bullet. He huddled in the cold cell and longed for home. Waves of fear swept over him but childhood memories strengthened him and brought him comfort. In his fatigue he drifted in and out of a fitful sleep broken by a confused jumble of emotions until he was too exhausted to worry any more. He resigned himself to possible torture and certain death, but not before he had given his captors a run for their money.

Des was like that. He had always had a sense of there being something bigger – as if someone bigger was nearby looking after him. This helped to give him an inner reserve of strength. Coupled with an ability to laugh at his circumstances with a humour that seemed to find something funny in the most difficult situation, Des was often able to rise above problems. These qualities drew people to him and he was liked and respected by many; and it was these very qualities that had led him into his present predicament for he had been one of the leaders of the most daring escape during the Second World War.

The cell grew cold and, huddled in the corner, at last he fell into sleep and dreamt of home.

Early Days

Desmond Lancelot Plunkett was born on 21st February 1915 in Guntur, in the Madras Presidency of India. His father, Arthur Lancelot Plunkett, was a distinguished civil engineer and worked for many years on the Madras Southern Maratta

The family car driven by Des's father.

Railways. He, too, had been born in India and this was later to cause some difficulty when Desmond wanted a British passport. His Scots mother, Margaret Robertson, gave birth to five sons and two daughters of whom Desmond was the eldest. His early schooling was in Scotland and then in Surrey where all the brothers were educated. While his father, Arthur Lancelot Bonner Plunkett, was employed from 1921 to 1923 as the Resident Engineer for Trinidad Land Reclamation Ltd. the family resided temporarily with their grandparents in Oban and Desmond attended school there. His grandfather, William Robertson, was an elder in the Presbyterian Church so there were no games on Sundays and discipline was strict but it was here that Desmond had his first grounding in the 'faith'. His grandfather would sit him on his knee and relate to him many of the Bible stories.

On his return from Trinidad his father became Chief Engineer in the office of Sir Douglas Fox & Partners in Westminster who were the designers for Dorman Long of the Sydney Harbour Bridge. The famous Sydney Harbour Bridge was, on completion, the longest cantilever bridge in the world. The family lived at Henley-on-Thames and at Esher in Surrey. During this time his father was admitted as a full member of the Institutes of Civil Engineers and Water Engineers.

In 1927 the whole family moved to the Bahamas for a year. Desmond went to school in a class which was all of African extraction and Desmond had his first contact with people who had originally come from the continent on which he would spend much of his life. Returning to England he attended school at Clarkes College in Surbiton for one term, then in 1929 he went on to Kings College at Wimbledon. Thirteen years later in 1942 his obituary was placed on the school roll of honour and remained there for many years:

Desmond Plunkett - Killed in Action - 1942.

Rossall School hockey team. Des back row, extreme right.

From Kings College he went to Rossall School where the very strict discipline hit him hard but where he flourished until his father's bankruptcy in 1932 which nearly ruined the family. When he had returned from the Bahamas Arthur Plunkett had accumulated a small fortune. At the time he was the youngest full member of the Institute of Civil Engineers but in 1932 he lost all his savings including a one hundred and ten acre estate at Hillerton Cross in Devonshire where the family had been living in a beautiful home, together with all the trappings of wealth from the butler to the chauffeur and some dozen other servants. The youngest children had a governess who came with a couple of prize Persian Blue cats complete with collars and leads. To add to their problems one night their home was gutted by fire which had started in the electricity generating plant. For a while the family lived on the insurance money paid out as compensation. After the estate had been put up for auction the family moved back to Surrey where they struggled from week to week on a hand to mouth basis. A Jewish barrister (Dan Rosenberg) was instrumental in helping them but Desmond had to find work. He had done well at all his various schools, having won the Victor Ludorum at his prep school and at Rossall seven prizes including one for Latin, as well as awards for hockey and swimming. Des was also a good boxer. When Des first went to Rossall School he had been aloof and proud but the boys there soon dealt with his attitude. Rossall was an Anglican Church school and the overall principles, discipline and standards left a lifetime impression on him. Des well remembers the early morning scramble for prayers. The morning bell would ring a slow toll which rapidly quickened into an urgent warning that all were expected in the chapel within minutes. Des would dive out of bed, dress and run down the stairs just in time to clash with a hundred other boys all trying to get through the chapel

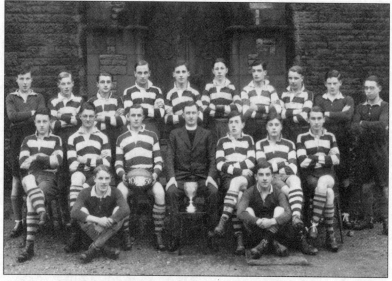

Rugby team. Des back row, second from right.

doors at the same time. He had a mischievous sense of humour and was well liked. However, because of the family bankruptcy his education was cut short a year earlier than intended and he left without sitting his Matric or School Certificate.

For a year he went to night school in Kingston but got nowhere with it. During this time he assisted his father in submitting tenders for the construction of dams in Egypt. In those days everything had to be worked out and laboriously written in longhand and Des helped with this. Without the proverbial backhander the tenders his father submitted for the first of the Aswan dams were unsuccessful for Arthur Plunkett would not compromise with bribes. Things got tough but Desmond wanted to fly and got a job in Hanworth for seven months working in the workshop of an aeronautical company called British Klemm which was building German planes made out of wood. They produced the Klemm Swallow amongst others. This was his first contact with a career that would make him into a bomber pilot.

Desmond went on to work at the Hawker Aircraft Company at Kingston-on-Thames which was engaged in the manufacture of the Hawker Hurricane which came into production along with the Supermarine Spitfire at that time. Desmond then joined the Parnall Aircraft Company, largely concerned with power controlled gun turrets fitted to the Boulton Paul Fighter and the Sunderland Flying Boat. His work at the Hawker company introduced him to the high standard of workmanship required for modern aircraft manufacture and the men he worked with influenced him greatly, not only through their precision tooling but by the great kindness they showed in treating him as a son.

Later he joined Robert Kronfelt and worked in his drawing office in Hanworth for a year, from 1936–37. Kronfelt was a Jew who had worked in Germany building gliders. After the First World War Germany had been prohibited from manufacturing

Des with a 'Klemm Eagle', Hanworth 1936.

powered aeroplanes and so the glider industry had grown. Kronfelt had got out of Germany when the Nazi party got in and started building gliders in England. One plane he built had an extended wing length of nearly a hundred feet and stood ten feet off the ground. He established the world gliding height record at 30,000 feet. At this time Des learnt a tremendous amount about the principles of flight. One of Des's fellow employees was a German-speaking Czech and Desmond also began to pick up a smattering of German. This man gave Des his first taste of anti-Semitism when one day he started swearing and cursing all the Jews in the world, blaming them for a recent air disaster, the crash of the German airship, the *Hindenburg*, on 6th May 1937 in America!

On Wings of Glory

'They will mount up with wings like eagles.'

Des flew for the first time in 1925 as a lad of ten. His family lived at Esher in Surrey and sometimes aircraft would fly over. Des watched enthralled, as they crawled across the sky, taking ages to get from one horizon to the other! One day two Avro 504 aircraft, biplanes used in the First World War, landed in a field near the house. The pilots offered joy rides, two passengers at a time, both in the rear cockpits. Des was determined to have a ride and pestered his parents. Eventually they gave him a ticket and he dashed off full of joy only to find that the ticket allowed him into the grounds and not onto the plane. He was heartbroken and ran after his parents, weeping bitterly. His father took pity on him and gave him the extra five shillings needed and with great fortune he was able to catch the last flight of the day. Wearing his dad's overcoat which came down to his ankles he was not even strapped into the rear cockpit as the plane bumped off down the field. With his heart pounding Des was in heaven. As the horizon tilted and the earth reeled below Des felt the thrill and freedom of flying and the twenty minute flight awakened a great desire within him – one day he would be a pilot.

It was in 1936 that Desmond first found his own wings and took to the air. Some friends took him to Redhill Flying Club where he flew four hours in a Gypsy 1 Moth at £2 an hour. He then joined the RAF Volunteer Reserve which opened up opportunities to learn to fly free of charge. As a member he earned £25 a year retaining fee and was also paid one shilling an hour plus travel expenses. This was vital cash for Desmond who had taken on the role of family breadwinner after the death of his father on 13th August 1937. Des had a kindly and patient instructor who had an even temperament and under whom Des

Climbing in Wales. Des front left.

blossomed. After just seven hours Des flew solo! Now he was away and the sky was the limit.

The RAF was an elite force with a high reputation. Its early pilots had fought the German pilots during the First World War and had achieved a distinguished record. In 1939 Des graduated as a Flying Instructor with the British Royal Air Force. He had become one of an elite band of flying men. His pay went up from £30 to £60 – a tremendous amount – and later he flew Hawker Harts all around southern England on cross-country exercises. Soon he had accumulated hundreds of flying hours and was known as a highly efficient instructor with an ability to anticipate problems before they occurred. Some students had serious accidents which taught Des a very real respect for what could go wrong and made him very cautious. RAF standards of training were exceptionally high and were so instilled into him at this time that they remained with him for the rest of his life.

He spent every spare minute flying but he was brought down to earth in an unmistakable fashion when during the war he was shot down over Europe. His flying career had led him into the war and into captivity and now into the hands of the Gestapo.

CHAPTER 2

War

'Though I walk through the valley of the
shadow of death I shall fear no evil.'

As he lay curled up on the floor of his cell his youthful days seemed so far off, yet he was only in his mid twenties. However, the war had exposed him to much hardship and conflict. So much had happened so quickly and now as a prisoner in enemy hands he was about to face the gravest danger of all. Would the Gestapo succeed in breaking his will, he wondered? As a prisoner Des found the confinement of his cell the most frightening thing to handle. After experiencing the incredible freedom of flying, the cell was a terrible restriction. He longed for a familiar object or friendly face but he was surrounded by the cruel realities of war and hatred. He would have to toughen up if he were to overcome his present conditions.

When hostilities broke out between Britain and Germany on 3rd September 1939 Des was still an instructor and as such was highly valued, having logged up several thousand flying hours. Despite his many requests for active duty he was retained for the first two years of the war as an instructor and trained many of the young recruits chosen as war pilots. Eventually, in 1941, he was approved for active duty and told that he was to be posted for training as a bomber pilot with the rank of Flight Lieutenant. Des's notification of posting came a few

War staff. Des second row, extreme right.

days before his wedding and both his fiancée and his family were very tearful. However, Des knew that the future would hold no meaning for him unless he personally contributed to the war effort. Many of his buddies had already paid the cost and Des was more and more convinced about his own commitment.

He was married to Patricia on 22nd November 1941. It was a typical war wedding and the ceremony was planned to fit in between his flying duties.

At the time he was on a training course at RAF Lynham and so he simply borrowed an Avro Tutor trainer biplane and flew across to Meir Airfield where he had been previously stationed and which was near to his in-laws' home. From there Des thumbed a lift with a group of factory workers who, when they heard he was about to be married, thrust a pint of Guinness into his hands and insisted he drink it, which he did as fast as he

Meir, Stoke on Trent.Training staff and pilots 1941.
Des front row, 4th from left.

could. Des was not used to drinking and by the time he arrived
at his bride's home the effect was unmistakable. His father-in-
law was a strict teetotaller and was shaken at the condition of
his soon to be son-in-law. Des only just made the ceremony. He
staggered in smelling of booze and in such a jovial frame of
mind that he was oblivious to the effect his appearance had on
all who had gathered.Although shocked they were nevertheless
relieved to see him for they were beginning to wonder whether
he had cancelled the date. Des wore his uniform and Patricia
looked radiant despite not having a wedding dress.After the
reception they were whisked away to the railway station for an
overnight honeymoon on the train.

Des completed most of his operational training and after
posting to RAF Wellesbourne Mountford was given a Wellington
crew to complete his final training; his first combat missions

Wellington Bomber.

were also the first of the '1000 Bomber' raids on Cologne and Essen. At this stage of the war, on average only about six trips were as many as any member of a bomber crew could expect to conduct without meeting some disaster. Each trip lasted from four to six hours. In some cases about fifteen flying hours was all some crew members were completing. Of the original course that Des attended which comprised twenty five men, mostly officers, only three survived the war.

Desmond was posted to RAF Marham in Norfolk and it was during his third trip out that disaster struck.

His Longest Day – 21st June 1942
It was on a mission to Emden, flying over enemy occupied Holland, that Des was shot down. He was co-pilot of a Stirling bomber with a crew of eight, part of the Goldcoast 218 Squadron. The Stirling was a beautiful plane to fly and it handled

superbly. It was the RAF's first four engine monoplane bomber. It was powered by four Bristol Hercules XI engines and was capable of carrying a massive bomb load of up to 14,000 lbs or 6,350 kg. It was armed with eight .303 machine guns, two in the forward and upper turrets and four in the tail turret. The Stirlings first went into action in February 1941 and were used throughout the war. It was also the first RAF aircraft to be fitted with 'OBOE' blind bombing equipment.

On this fateful night they took off from Marham in Norfolk, near Kings Lynn, and headed for Europe which was in the grip of the Nazis. The night was bright and they crossed the Channel with no difficulty but Des had a strong premonition that he would not be returning. As they flew into enemy territory the nerves of all the crew were on edge.

Suddenly a crew member broke the tension. His frantic shouts could not disguise his fear. 'Searchlights and flak up ahead,' he screamed.

'Shut up,' snapped Des, having already seen the action.

They dodged through the German defences, reached Emden and lined up on target.

'Bombs away,' shouted the navigator and twenty seven cans of incendiary bombs plummeted down.

Swinging back they made for home but instead of first flying north over the Friesland Islands and North Sea as briefed the senior skipper decided to take a more direct route. After forty five minutes on the home run their peace was suddenly shattered by the warning cry of the rear gunner followed immediately by bursts of gun fire. A twin-engined German Messerschmidt fighter plane had appeared from nowhere and its shells ripped through the fuselage at 45 degrees upwards. The bomber shook under the impact but the firing ceased as the fighter sped beneath them. An inner fuel tank and the port wing had caught fire. Turning sharply, the fighter lined up about

400 metres directly behind them and let rip with a barrage of shells into the starboard wing and engines. A shell burst the inner fuel tank and the wing exploded in fire.

The skipper, an older man who had cribbed his age in order to get into combat, lost his nerve. It was his first taste of action in command of a Stirling and when the surprise attack hit he went into shock and froze, unable to take evasive action. They were a sitting duck. The German Messerschmidt 110 made three passes at them, each time with its guns blazing. After the starboard wing ignited the pilot battled with the controls for as long as he could but the furnace engulfed the wing and made the plane uncontrollable; it began to buckle and dive. Smoke filled the cabin and the pilot gave him the thumbs down sign which was the go ahead to bale out. Would there be time, Des wondered, to get out before the whole thing exploded or hit the ground. Des tried to rise from his seat but had forgotten to disentangle himself from the oxygen line and intercom plug. Frantically he clawed them off and as he climbed from the cockpit and struggled through the heat and smoke Des prayed:

'Lord Jesus, do I have to die now?'

He crawled down the stairs to find the hatch already open which gave him the precious extra moments he needed to get out. The gunner from the front turret was struggling to put on his parachute. In the terror of the moment time seemed to stand still. He had never in his life jumped from a plane and as he leapt into the empty sky he clung to his rip-cord but the force of air whipped his hands apart and yanked the parachute open. For a frightful moment Des thought he must have got snagged on the tail of the plane. Two seconds later he was hanging free and watched the giant Stirling turn on its back and nosedive to its grave. It hit the earth with a loud explosion in a ball of flames. Three of the crew, including the skipper, failed to get out.

'What a waste,' he thought to himself as it exploded. A Stirling bomber cost in the region of about £70,000 sterling. The German Messerschmidt 110 was flown by Hauptman Ludwig Becker who according to records claimed the Stirling as his thirty third victim. High above, the German Messerschmidt 110 was firing at another British bomber. The engines screamed as the bomber dodged and twisted and then finally got away. As it was midsummer and drifting at 16,000 feet Des looked down on a landscape bathed in midsummer light. In fact it was the early hours of the morning and up in the air it was getting quite bright, almost like broad daylight!

Desmond watched the victorious German plane as it circled him in the early morning light. He hung, helpless and exposed. It was not unknown for airmen to be shot out of the sky as they descended by parachute. Des wondered whether he could expect a burst of fire to rip through him but Becker was a gentleman and flew off after other prey.

Everything became very quiet as Des floated in the air and there were long moments to admire the beauty of the view. The action packed, explosive last few moments seemed to accentuate the silence. All of a sudden the war seemed a long way off and the Dutch countryside beneath him lay bathed in peace, stretched out like a painting. The fields looked like stamps with quaint villages breaking the patterns. However, the picturesque landscape masked a sinister presence – the Nazis were in full force and held the country in their vice-like stranglehold. Soon the feeling of peace was gone for good and Des found himself at the start of a long and arduous ordeal.

Capture
He landed safely but could not see any other surviving crew members. He would never meet any of them again, except one man called Reg Attwood who was the radio operator and who was the last to get out just before the plane flipped on its back.

Des met him years later at a POW reunion in Salisbury, Rhodesia (now Harare, Zimbabwe). Des landed in a beautiful green field with soft turf and a herd of cows which in their curiosity came to investigate him as he lay stunned in the grass. He did not have long to relax. He was a few hundred metres from the bomber which was now burning fiercely. The ammunition it contained began to explode spasmodically and in his dazed bewilderment he thought it was the whole German army coming to get him. His mind began to race as he imagined what could happen if they caught him. He gathered up the parachute, hid it in a hole, and remembering his instructions to get away from the landing spot as quickly as possible, he began to run as fast as he could. He found a country lane and kept running. When a group of Dutchmen came down the road he paused long enough to hide in the ditch to avoid them. He crossed several fields and dykes and waded through thick mud. The land was flat with few trees and very little cover in which to hide. He was exhausted and so he curled up in a corner of a field. He had no emergency rations and nothing to keep himself warm, was cold, disorientated and alone. He wondered why he had escaped death – all he had to show for his misfortune was a small scratch on his face.

Airmen who suddenly found themselves stranded miles from help experienced tremendous trauma. One day they would be safe in their familiar surroundings and the following day they would find themselves cut off and isolated deep in hostile territory.

The new day was Sunday 21st June and Des was surprised to see a group of men, all dressed up in their Sunday togs, walking through the fields inspecting their crops. Covered in mud, he felt a wave of embarrassment mixed with the fear of discovery well up in him. He fell to the ground and crawled away.

The day wore on and Des realised his hopeless plight. There was little chance of getting out of enemy occupied Holland. He had no supplies and no idea where to get help. He spent the day hiding and in the evening, while it was still light, made his way to a nearby village called Wognum. A number of people immediately recognised him as a British airman – he was very conspicuous as he was wearing a white British Air Force pullover covered with mud. The people spoke to him and calmed his fears, assuring him he was in no danger, but they called the village Burgomaster who explained to Des that there was no way they could help him evade capture. Too many people had seen him and it would be impossible to hide him. It was just a matter of time and rather than endanger others he had no alternative other than to give himself up. Although his attitude was one of sympathy and concern there was nothing that could be done. Des reluctantly agreed and in trepidation waited for the German authorities to arrive. They showed no sympathy at all, threw him into the back of an open car, and took him to a nearby Luftwaffe station.

'Where did you drop your bombs?' they asked.

'On Emden,' Des replied.

One man threw up his arms in rage and despair.

'That is where my family lives!' he cried.

Des was fortunate to have bailed out over Holland. Airmen who came down in more hostile areas were often badly treated and even killed before they ever got to a POW camp. Hitler had given orders that civilians should be encouraged to lynch all airmen on capture.

The next day he was taken to a jail in Amsterdam and put with about fifteen other airmen who had also been shot down. Later they were moved to an interrogation and transit camp called Dulag Luft near Frankfurt-on-Maine. This was the beginning of an experience that nearly cost him his life and, except for a short time on the run as a fugitive, he was to remain a prisoner until the end of the war in 1945. It was not long after his capture that his first child, a daughter, was born, but Des had started a long personal fight, a fight for survival.

POW

Des and about fifty other POWs were taken in a crowded railway carriage from Holland deep into the heart of enemy territory to a POW camp at Sagan called Stalag Luft III. The journey took several days. Food and water was scarce. Being an officer Des was put in charge of some of the POWs during the journey and had his time cut out keeping their spirits up. On arrival at Sagan they were marched off to the camp which already held several thousand prisoners, mainly Air Force personnel. Many well known airmen were at this camp. One of them was the famous Battle of Britain pilot Douglas Bader. He had lost both his legs in a pre-war flying accident but this did not deter him from becoming a fighter pilot. He simply had two artificial limbs fitted and this astounded the Germans when he was shot down.

Stalag Luft III was a dismal place. The camp was set in a clearing in a thick pine forest and comprised a number of low barracks and huts surrounded by high barbed wire fences. It covered about half or three-quarters of a square mile and the servicemen were housed in different compounds. Sentry boxes on tall poles stood at strategic spots around the camp. Life in the camp was by no means easy but there was a certain code of conduct among the prisoners and their captors. The Geneva Convention laid down conditions under which POWs were to be treated. Unfortunately these were not always observed but it was understood that to escape was an honourable aim for POWs and many of them were anxious to do so. This was because of the realization amongst them of the high cost of their training and the hours that it had taken to put them into service. Consequently it became a high priority to escape. There

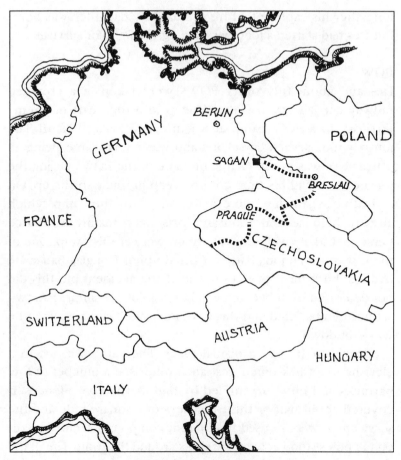

Map of Central Europe.

was always some plan for the next attempt either by individuals or in groups. To counter these attempts special German guards known among the prisoners as 'ferrets' were permanently on the prowl and could appear at any moment. They would seek out tunnels and watch closely for unusual behaviour. This made the task of escaping especially difficult.

As soon as Des arrived at Stalag Luft III Douglas Bader and

another fighter pilot prisoner, Stanford Tuck, got hold of him and for a long while grilled him with questions about the war and home. They were starved of news and hungry for information. Des shared his room with a number of interesting men. Tim Wahlemn had experienced some bad luck. Des had met him before the war at Hanworth Aerodrome where they had both trained. Tim and his crew had got lost in bad weather and they had been forced to land their Wellington on an airfield in France where they were captured and he was so embarrassed about it. Tim had worked in a bank in London before he joined the elite RAF; he was to become a skilled forger of documents and produced many that were used by those who escaped. They

POW: Flight Lieutenant Desmond Plunkett.

became close friends. Tony Hayter also became a close friend and assisted Des in the printing of maps to be used in their escape. He had been shot down in North Africa. Gordon Brettell was caught when he bailed out of his Spitfire while returning to England after escorting American B17s. He had run out of fuel and landed in the sea off the north coast of France. Another POW, known as Cassie, was a South African from Cape Town and a great actor and artist. Digger Carter from New Zealand was shot down while on a bombing raid over Germany. Tim, Tony and Gordon were all to escape with Des but Des was the only one to survive. Another close friend of Des's was a Czech pilot called Ernie Valenta. He was one of the first to escape but he too was to die.

Des made several attempts to get away. His first plan was to get into a cart removing ash from the camp. He and his good friend Ivo Tonder, a Czech pilot who had joined the RAF, climbed into the cart and were covered with ash by a friend. Unfortunately the coals beneath them were still hot and after a while they were unable to endure the heat. They sprang out with their 'pants on fire' and the onlookers had a good laugh. Two rather sorry, ashen faced and scalded men abandoned their bid for freedom and limped back to their hut to wash. The second attempt was when Des and Ivo tried to escape through a 'mole tunnel'. A mole tunnel was a tunnel dug from within the trench that encircled the camp just inside the outside fence. This trench was dug by the Germans to prevent tunnels from within the camp getting out. The idea was that tunnels dug from within the camp would hit the trench and thereby be exposed. However, would-be escapers simply crawled into the trench and started digging from there instead of from further back under a hut. Certain spots in the trench could not be seen from the 'Goon Boxes' which were the raised guard houses built every 100 metres and which straddled the outer fence. On this occasion two diggers had got into the trench undetected and after digging all day had reached the outside wire by midnight. All that was now needed was for the last few feet to be opened and the tunnel was ready. Des and Ivo were included in the escape bid and were getting ready to leave when the German guard dogs sniffed out the tunnel.

Not to be put off, another plan was initiated. Long, light-weight ladders were constructed from the beading in one of the passages in the hut and these were buried just outside the barracks until they could be used. Early morning mist was quite common, especially in winter, and under this cover it was considered they could get over the outer fence without being spotted. Once again the guards found the ladders before the mist came. Des then helped with another tunnel which was dug from under one of the huts. He and Jimmy James were part of a team that worked on it and it got to about 18 metres out when it hit a sewage works which poured into the tunnel and they abandoned the attempt.

Operation Escape 200

After this Roger Bushell, who was in charge of organising escapes, told Des to give up tunnelling and concentrate on map making. He needed someone who was a draughtsman and able to head a team to produce hundreds of detailed maps required for the mass escape which he was planning. Some 2,500 maps were eventually produced. Each escape bid had to be approved by the camp escape committee which was made up of senior officers. Roger Bushell's plan was so good that it received full support. He guaranteed Des an opportunity to get out through one of the tunnels he proposed to dig in 1943.

Bushell's plan was to dig a tunnel from which a mass escape could take place. It was code named Operation Escape 200 as it was intended that two hundred prisoners should get out through it. And so Des became involved in the largest ever POW break-out during the entire war.

It was also from this camp that another famous escape, known as the 'Wooden Horse', took place. In this escape three men got out through a tunnel dug beneath a gymnastic vaulting box which was carried out every day and placed in exactly the same spot. From beneath this box, day after day, the secret tunnel was dug. This was a much shorter tunnel than Bushell's because of the advantage it had of starting nearer to the outer fence. It was dug right under the very noses both of the ferrets and of the guards in the goon box and was an extraordinary achievement. In October 1943 three POWs got out through this tunnel and all three made it back home via Sweden.

However, Roger Bushell's tunnel was to be a mass escape and was intentionally planned as such to cause as much confusion as possible to the Germans. It was the longest tunnel ever dug, being about three hundred and sixty feet long and nearly thirty feet underground. The tunnel took the combined skills of many hundred men and a full year's preparation. It also gave the men something to work for and kept their minds active during the long hours of confinement. Many nationalities were imprisoned at Sagan and there was an almost unlimited number of skills which were used with great effect in constructing the tunnel.

When captured men were first restricted many of them had an intense desire to be free and felt like trapped animals. The intensity of this urge diminished in time but was exacerbated by the uncertainty of how long they would have to remain as prisoners. This sometimes caused prisoners to behave in both humorous and tragic ways. Some of the POWs were daredevils and took unnecessary risks. Around the camp perimeter was a 'warning wire' which was about half a metre high and ran parallel with the outer fence. This marked the off-limit zone and anyone who crossed this wire was gunned down. To escape the boredom of camp life there were nevertheless those who risked a bullet by crossing the line. Some prisoners had such mental turmoil that they were unable to continue living under the circumstances and found methods to end it all. Other prisoners deliberately thought up ways that would rile their captors. One prankster, Murdoch MacDonald, observed how the German guards were constantly scrutinizing the camp through their binoculars and hit on a plan to upset them. He found two small dark coloured Nugget shoepolish tins and carefully cut holes in the middle of them through which he could look. Finding a not too obvious spot he sat down and held the tins to his eyes, and proceeded to mimic the guards by viewing them as if through binoculars. It was not long before he was noticed and some confusion broke out amongst the soldiers. An indignant group of officers descended upon the camp and sought out Murdoch, demanding to know from where he had got the binoculars. In exaggerated innocence he denied all knowledge of them but eventually the tins were brought out and shown to the irate officials. The prisoners all had a laugh at their expense.

The camp theatre was active in organising entertainment and debating evenings and religious services were also held. Murdoch MacDonald was a Presbyterian minister and was highly regarded by the men. He held services in the camp and spoke with such conviction and persuasion that many prisoners came to listen to him speak.

A camp orchestra also practised in the theatre. But the theatre was to prove helpful in another way - large quantities of sand from the tunnel were to be hidden under its floor.

CHAPTER 3

A Tunnel Called Harry

*'Give heed to my cry for I am brought very low; Deliver
me from my persecutors for they are too strong for me.'*

Bushell's plan was to build three tunnels, Tom, Dick and
Harry. It was through the tunnel called Harry that Des had
escaped. Seventy six men got out of Stalag Luft III and it was
Des's escape and subsequent capture that had landed him in
Gestapo custody. Held by the Gestapo in solitary confinement,
Des's fate hung in the balance. The threat of execution was part
of the psychological preparation for the interrogation that was
to follow. The cell into which he had been thrown was located
within the bowels of Pankratz Gaol which was infamous during
the Second World War for its awful conditions. Des had plenty of
time to reflect on his situation and to prepare himself for the
coming ordeal. How was he to cope with Gestapo methods and
more especially, how could he cover for the many people who
had been involved with the escape? He went over the events
again and again in his mind and perfected his story until he
could repeat it without flaw. It was this amazing ability to
remember small details and to remain calm under pressure that
was to stand Des in good stead in the days ahead.

The man in overall charge of the escape was Roger Bushell
who was a South African born in Hermanus in the Cape. He was
trained as a barrister and could speak several languages
including English, Afrikaans, German, Czech, French and Xhosa.

He could quote Shakespeare in German. He was a squadron leader in the South African 92 (Hurricane) Squadron. He arrived in the summer of 1942 and was in bad shape, having been through a gruelling time including nine months solitary confinement. He had escaped several times before and the Gestapo had warned him that if he did once more he would be shot. This did not deter him from setting in motion yet another plan to escape. There had been many attempts by prisoners to tunnel out of the camps but these were groups of men working independently. Roger proposed that there should be a combined effort which if successful would allow two hundred men to

The trolley system.

make a bid for freedom. He motivated the men to begin to work as a team and encouraged them to make a collective effort at a mass escape which would catch the Germans when they least expected it. He argued that it was part of their duty and contribution to the war effort.

His plan was to dig three tunnels and if one or two were discovered then there would be the third to fall back on. Tom was indeed discovered and Dick became a hide for tools and equipment. It was to be Harry that would be the route to freedom. Harry was dug from under a hut and was 363 feet long. The tunnel was an engineering marvel, considering the conditions under which the men had to work.

The man in charge of planning and constructing the tunnel was a Canadian called Wally Floody. He was also one of the main diggers. He was a large man of six feet three inches and spent many long hours underground. Twice he was nearly killed when the tunnel collapsed on him. On the one occasion he was buried under a ton of sand and only frantic digging by his friends got him out in time. On the other occasion he was crawling naked through the tunnel when a section collapsed onto him. Fortunately his face was by a ventilation shaft, which enabled him to breathe, but it took over an hour to get him out! Wally never had the opportunity to escape through the tunnel because he was suspected by the camp security officials of planning an escape and he was transferred to another compound at Bellaria some three miles away. This no doubt saved him from the fate of so many of his colleagues.

Harry was dug from under the stove of hut 104. To enter the tunnel the stove had to be carefully removed and then replaced with no outward evidence of disturbance. The tunnel was strengthened with planks taken from all around the camp buildings and a ventilation system with bellows was set up as well as lights and a trolley system on rails. Large amounts of

Interior of camp hut. Left to right: Des, Tim Walenn, Bourman, Carter, Valenta, Davis, Griffiths.

sand had to be dispersed without detection. It was this sand that made tunnelling so difficult because it was prone to collapse and trap diggers underground. It was also hard to hide because it was brilliant white and unmistakable. The tunnel was dug thirty feet underground to foil the ferrets who were experts at discovering shallow tunnels. They had set up monitors all around the camp that could detect any vibrations caused by digging but these did not work with deep tunnels. The combined skills of several hundred men were employed in the project and strict co-ordination, discipline and security had to be maintained for it to be a success. As well as the tunnel, other preparations had to be made. Civilian clothes had to be fabricated, maps and travel and identity documents had to be forged, compasses made, and money and food obtained. Roger and the escape committee did not overlook anything and detailed plans were made to cover every aspect.

Roger was a man of many talents and a born leader who gathered men around him and inspired them to great achievements. He had great vision and courage and was never daunted by the circumstances or the size of the task. He also seemed to know the Germans better than they knew themselves. He was always one jump ahead of them and anticipated their every move. He was able to acquire inside information and had such good contacts that he could tell the German officers and their NCOs when the Gestapo would conduct their surprise searches. He would warn them to get rid of all their incriminating evidence such as chocolate, Nescafé and other items that they had traded from the POW Red Cross parcels. He would also warn them when the homes of their mistresses were about to be searched. If the Gestapo found any suspicious items it would be enough to send the men to the Russian front and his early warnings had saved several German officers from trouble

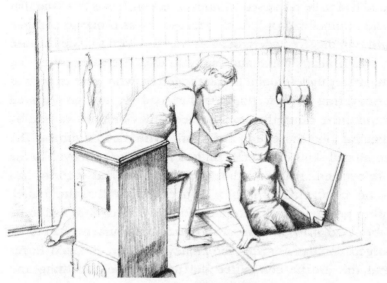

Descending the tunnel.

so they were very appreciative. Roger had developed good relations with some Germans who could foresee that the Allies would eventually defeat Germany. Many of the Germans were in his confidence and he used them to great advantage in obtaining information and items required for the tunnel. Once a German had helped the POWs Roger would be completely ruthless with him and insist that he should continue to assist them. If there was any reluctance Roger threatened to report him and get him sent to the Russian war front. They highly respected Roger. One day a German guard brought in a desperately needed transformer for use by the prisoners. Because he had been away on leave he returned just as the Gestapo were conducting one of their surprise raids. He carried the bulky item in through the main gates but could not leave it in his room for fear that it would be discovered. He immediately contacted Roger's men and asked to unload it but Roger told him they had nowhere to put it and he must sweat it out until the danger was past. So as the Gestapo searched everywhere for contraband a German officer carried this heavy transformer intended for the prisoners all around camp so as to elude them. Eventually Roger sent for it and relieved the German of his burden!

Because Des had previous experience in draughtsmanship he was put in charge of one of the most important aspects of the escape. He headed up a team of about fourteen men who produced the maps to be used in the escape. They bribed a German guard who got them a large detailed map of Europe which was then meticulously copied in sections. Des used a novel method to reproduce the maps. The prisoners were fortunate enough to receive Red Cross parcels in which there were packets of crystal jelly. By washing the crystals in water they were able to dissolve the sugar and were left with gelatine. They then carefully constructed some shallow trays using tins which were joined by resin obtained from the nearby fir trees.

POWs in camp. Left to right: Iowitt, Des, Valenta, Griffiths.

Once the jelly had separated it was poured into these pans to set in thin layers. The original map was then hand copied in five colours and was placed on top of the gelatine and pressed onto it so that it absorbed the inks. From this template up to twenty five further copies could be reproduced. In all, over 2,500 maps were printed using this method. Tony Hayter, John Hartnell-Beavis and Kolonovsky, a Pole who had worked in a Polish cartography office prior to capture, were the mainstay of the mapping team.

The map team produced a large map of Europe and hung it up in one of the rooms. Little coloured flags marked the various front line positions of the Allied armies. The camp chief of security, a German called Glemwitz, would often visit the prisoners unannounced. In order to forewarn the mapping team of the approach of any officers or guards a number of lookouts were stationed at strategic spots. When danger approached the warning cry would go something like, 'Look out, the kettle is boiling.' Not only was Glemwitz very observant but he also had a sense of humour. He would approach the hut proclaiming loudly that the kettle was boiling. He would also examine the map with its various flags and make suitable corrections.

'Herr Plunkett,' he would say, 'there is an error,' and then proceeded to point out the mistakes thereby unwittingly assisting the mappers.

Most of the maps were highly detailed to the scale of 1:2500. Bibles were also sent in the Red Cross parcels and these Bibles had protective, transparent covers which Des used to copy the original map. Thus the Bibles did not only point the way spiritually but became a practical means to show the way to those who did eventually escape.

Escape to Victory

After much preparation the day for the great escape arrived. The plan was to get two hundred men out through the tunnel and each was allocated a number which placed him in line for the escape. Clothes made from uniforms had been dyed and altered so as to pass for civilian clothes. Forged papers, maps, travel documents, money and permits were all supplied.

Nerves became tense as last minute details were finalised. Each man had to have an escape route worked out with suitable contacts and a plausible strategy. Sagan was situated in the heart of Nazi territory and hundreds of miles would have to be covered. The men made final plans with one another, farewells were said and arrangements made as to how they would meet up after it was all over. For most of them their farewells were final – it would be the last time they would ever see each other. Rumours were that the Nazis had been ordered to shoot all escapers when caught and this knowledge tended to put the

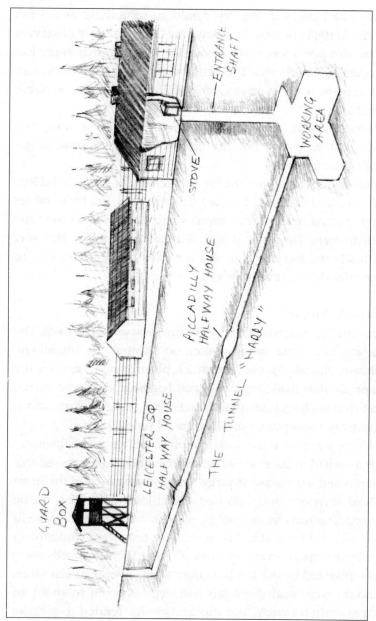

Sectional drawing of escape tunnel 'Harry'.

men more on edge. These rumours were confirmed to Des years later in Calcutta, India, where he was reunited with a fellow prisoner, Bill Gummer. Bill was the son of a Norwegian father and a Scots mother and was fluent in several languages. Consequently he was the camp interpreter and as such had access to the admin. block. One day he walked in to find that both the office and the safe of the camp Commandant were open. Sifting through the papers he came upon a top secret communiqué from Hitler. Known as the Kugel Order or Bullet Order, it was a directive that all Air Force escapers were to be shot. Hitler had taken an intense dislike to the Allied Air Force. It was hitting him too hard and too close to home. Not only that but every time the airmen broke out of the camps they caused a lot of difficulties within Germany.

On the evening of 24th March 1944 two hundred men

POWs. Left to right: Valenta, Zaplati, Busina, Bently, Tonder, Des, Cigos.

crowded into Hut 104 and prepared to make their way through the tunnel to freedom. They had congregated within the hut without drawing the attention of any of the guards. There was not a spare inch to move! All their combined work and carefully laid plans for freedom were about to pay off. However, lasting freedom would not be easy for many miles of enemy territory lay between the men and home. It was a bold undertaking. Des was allocated number thirteen out of the tunnel. Nobody else wanted the number so Des volunteered for it, knowing that it would put him right up near the start of the escape and give him added time to get away. He teamed up with a Czech friend Bedrich (Freddie) Dvorak who was number fourteen. After many adventures Des and Freddie were eventually caught. They were the last of the prisoners to be recaptured. Out of the seventy six men who got out only three made it to freedom. Des and Freddie were caught a day's travel from the Swiss border on Easter Saturday 1944 but they had spent two weeks outwitting the national alert that mobilised the biggest manhunt of the war.

As the men waited for their turn down the tunnel there were delays caused by difficulty opening the exit as well as a blackout brought on by an air raid. The Allied aircraft were usually welcomed by the POWs but tonight they were not wanted. They were causing too much of a delay and the prisoners were losing precious time. At long last Des was down the tunnel and being propelled along its narrow confines on the trolley system. Two rails had been laid the entire length of the tunnel and on this a trolley with pulleys had been installed. Lights powered from the main electrical supply of the camp lit up the tunnel from start to finish and ventilator pipes brought in fresh air. The tunnel was constructed in sections with 'stations' in between which allowed room for halts. The tunnel itself was only about two feet square in size and there was no spare room for bulky kit. Only a bare minimum of luggage could be taken by each man. The men

At the wire.

had to stretch out flat on the trolley and cling to it as it was hauled through the tunnel. Des reached the first station called 'Piccadilly' and was soon rattling along to 'Leicester Square'. At last he found himself squeezed into the exit chamber with a number of others waiting for the all clear signal. At his turn he climbed the thirty foot ladder to the exit. As he stuck his head out he felt the cool night air on his face and breathed in the fresh air with a sense of relief from the stifling heat of the tunnel. The exit had fallen short of the intended distance and was only about twenty five metres from the guard box overlooking the whole area. Great care had to be taken not to alert the guards as they patrolled the fence. Fortunately the spotlights pointed back into the camp and the outside area was in darkness. A warning system had been rigged up with a long string from the exit to the edge of the woods where the last man out of the tunnel waited to give the signal. The aim was to keep the men moving as fast as possible but without arousing the suspicions of the guards. The tug on the string gave Des the go ahead and he quietly crawled across the open ground to the undergrowth. At last he was outside the dreaded wire and felt a great personal victory over the enemy. He had achieved what had been his dream since capture – he was free. He was past the first barrier but many hundreds of miles lay ahead. It was about 11.00 pm and he was at the start of an epic journey right through the heartland of the Third Reich.

Fast Train to Freedom

Immediately after getting out of the tunnel Freddie and Des headed for the local railway station, as did all the first forty escapers. These were especially selected because they were experienced escapers able to speak a European language. Des had learnt some German, as well as some French at school. Freddie, being a Czech, spoke Czech perfectly. These were the prisoners who had the best chance of catching the train and making a speedy get-away from the vicinity of the camp. From previous experience escaped prisoners had found that the trains were the best means of moving rapidly through Europe. Those who attempted to travel by other means had little chance of getting far.

The spring thaw had not yet started and snow lay thick on the ground. The two men walked through the forest that surrounded the prison camp and made their way towards Sagan station. They skirted around a band of Russian POWs who were working on the line, and entered the station through the subway just as an air raid siren sounded. They bought two tickets from a ticket machine but the woman ticket collector refused to allow them on to the platform and told them to get down to the bomb shelter. At that moment a large German Warrant Officer thumped Des roughly on his back, dispatching him to the shelter. Freddie followed but grabbed Des's arm at the announcement of the arrival on platform 3 of the train to Breslau, their first stop. Leaving the entrance to the shelter they doubled up the stairs just as the train came to a stop. Out stepped a high ranking German officer in uniform and accosted Des.

'Ist gerade Luftalarm?' (Is there an air raid warning here?)

'Jawohl.' (Yes.)

Des replied as casually as it was possible in the circumstances.

They slipped past the man and jumped through the open door, closing it firmly behind them. Because of the air raid the train did not delay and in less than a few minutes they were moving rapidly away from Sagan. It was a fast train travelling at seventy to eighty miles an hour and the sound of the wheels and the movement of the carriage speeding along brought them a sense of comfort as every moment took them further away from the dangers of the camp and the tension of the escape. Roger had warned them to catch the first train out regardless of its destination as long as it was going away from Sagan and put as much distance as possible between them and the camp because as soon as the escape was discovered thousands of German soldiers would be looking for them. They stood in the corridor in total darkness because the train was blacked out owing to the air raid. The light reflected from the snow outside caught the tense outline of their faces. They were under tremendous stress. Freddie was convinced that they should not be found with the tickets purchased at Sagan in case the tunnel had been discovered and the alert given. After ten minutes he had persuaded Des and they threw the tickets out of the window. While standing in the corridor Roger Bushell came up and without saying a word squeezed their hands and passed on. He actually walked the entire length of the train to ascertain how many POWs had caught it. After forty minutes the train slowed down and stopped at Legnitz where they briefly disembarked. The platform was full of hundreds of men in uniform so they hastily got back on again and soon the train was back to top speed. They managed to find an empty compartment and settled down to contemplate the situation. No sooner had they settled down than a verbal tide of abuse came from the next compartment. They listened aghast as a German woman from Berlin described the sobering details of Allied bombing on the city. She declared her avowed intention of what she would do if ever she got her hands on the murderous 'Terror Fliegers' who were responsible.

From August 1942 to March 1944 the Allied Air Forces had relentlessly bombed the centre of Berlin city and other cities in an attempt to inflict maximum damage right to the heart of the Nazi war machine. Over 30,000 tons of bombs had been dropped and caused devastating destruction. But it had cost the Allies dearly; they had lost 600 planes and their crews. POW camps were rapidly filling up. Now two of these bomber pilots sat within earshot of a woman distraught over the loss of her loved ones. The two men sank deeper in their seats and soberly contemplated the horrors of the bombs that had fallen. They also reflected on the soldiers that crowded the platform at Legnitz. Most of them were wounded, some with bandaged heads and limbs and many on crutches. Evidently the war was hitting them hard.

Des and Freddie got off at Breslau and wondered how they would explain the loss of their tickets to the ticket collector. As they approached the exit they found a heated discussion in progress between the ticket collector and a German traveller and in the distraction they slipped through unnoticed. What marvellous timing, Des thought. Mingling with the crowd, they walked past the sleepy Gestapo police, through the gates into the main hall and up to the notice board to work out the next leg of their journey. They were feeling elated and could not believe that they had travelled as guests of Hitler from Sagan to Breslau for the cost of two pfennigs (about two pence).

CHAPTER 4

On the Run in the Biggest Manhunt in Germany

'For in the day of trouble He will conceal me in His shelter, in the secret of His tent He will hide me.'

Their next destination was Glatz where they sat in the cold hall for about five hours until 6.00 am waiting for the next train. They were tired but unable to sleep. The hall was crowded with soldiers mainly going to the Russian front. At about 2.00 am they saw a fellow prisoner, Van der Stock, walking down the centre of the hall and a little later he returned in the opposite direction. Van der Stock was one of the three to make it back to Britain. Other escaped prisoners were there too. Flight Lieutenant Rupert Stevens and Lt. Johannes Gouws of the South African Air Force were waiting on the other side of the hall. Both were to perish at the hands of the Gestapo. They saw Roger, who approached them and asked in French for a cigarette light. They talked softly. Roger had teamed up with a French prisoner called Bernard Scheidhauer who was spending every spare moment catching up with pleasures he had missed in camp. It was the last contact they had with Roger who told them there were only a few prisoners left on the train and that he was about to return all the way back to Sagan and then go on to France. Roger Bushell and Bernard Scheidhauer made it back through Sagan despite the heavy presence of police who were by then alerted country-wide. The Gestapo never suspected that they would return but were stopping scores of travellers who had incorrect papers. Bushell and Scheidhauer made it to Saarbrucken on the French border where they were stopped at a police check point. Everything was in order but as they passed through one policemen fired a question in English; Scheidhauer answered in English and they were caught. This was their death knell. Roger had escaped before and been free in Czechoslovakia for about a year living with a friend called Zaphie. He and Zaphie had been caught and the Gestapo had told the men that next time they would be shot. Zaphie never did attempt another escape and survived. Des met him after the war at Cosford where they were both de-briefed. He was a broken man. All his family had been killed by the Gestapo. The Gestapo kept their word – both Roger Bushell and Bernard Scheidhauer were shot soon after capture.

Des and Freddie sat in the station hall and read the propaganda notices pinned up on the walls.

'Ist Ihre Reise für den Sieg notwendig?' (Is your journey really necessary for Victory?)

They felt theirs certainly was!

Another said, *'Alle Räder müssen für den Sieg rollen.'* (All wheels must roll for Victory.) The quicker these wheels start rolling the better, thought Des.

Just before 6.00 am an announcement was made requesting the Gestapo officers immediately to go to the main office. The announcement was unnerving. Something was up, so the two men left the hall and made their way to the platform. Soon the train arrived and they boarded and were on their way to the town of Glatz. Their compartment was full and a German opened conversation with Des. This proved most embarrassing as all Des could mumble was something about the weather being cold which was not very profound for that time of year. Eventually the German gave up, probably in disgust, and the two

To all Prisoners of War!

The escape from prison camps is no longer a sport!

Germany has always kept to the Hague Convention and only punished recaptured prisoners of war with minor disciplinary punishment.

Germany will still maintain these principles of international law.

But England has besides fighting at the front in an honest manner instituted an illegal warfare in non combat zones in the form of gangster commandos, terror bandits and sabotage troops even up to the frontiers of Germany.

They say in a captured secret and confidential English military pamphlet.

THE HANDBOOK
OF MODERN IRREGULAR
WARFARE:

". . . the days when we could practise the rules of sportsmanship are over. For the time being, every soldier must be a potential gangster and must be prepared to adopt their methods whenever necessary."

"The sphere of operations should always include the enemy's own country, any occupied territory, and in certain circumstances, such neutral countries as he is using as a source of supply."

England has with these instructions opened up a non military form of gangster war!

Germany is determined to safeguard her homeland, and especially her war industry and provisional centres for the fighting fronts. Therefore it has become necessary to create strictly forbidden zones, called death zones, in which all unauthorised trespassers will be immediately shot on sight.

Escaping prisoners of war, entering such death zones, will certainly lose their lives. They are therefore in constant danger of being mistaken for enemy agents or sabotage groups.

Urgent warning is given against making future escapes!

In plain English: Stay in the camp where you will be safe! Breaking out of it is now a damned dangerous act.

The chances of preserving your life are almost nil!

All police and military guards have been given the most strict orders to shoot on sight all suspected persons.

Escaping from prison camps has ceased to be a sport!

men dozed. They had not slept for thirty six hours. At Glatz they caught a slow train to Bad Reinertz, a holiday spa in the mountains. This train was full of happy holiday-makers with bags of gear and the two men longed to change places and forget that they were on the run. The skies were blue but the snow lay thick on the ground. They imagined skiing down the slopes to freedom. It was quite strange how on the first day after their escape from a POW camp they were on their way to a holiday camp! They arrived at their destination and it certainly was a very nice and luxurious place. Des went off to the toilets to relieve himself.

He was bursting and when finished he sighed with relief and said out loud in English, 'That's better.'

To his horror he had not seen a German standing in the next cubicle who nearly fell over backward, and stared at him aghast.

Des beat a quick retreat before the German could react, with Freddie swearing at him in Czech. They hastily left the building and fortunately it started to snow heavily which completely enveloped them. By the time the snow eased they were over a small hill and out of sight with their tracks obliterated, preventing anyone following them.

Using their map they trudged over the snow-covered hills. The scene had a fairy-like quality with snow piled up against the houses but as they climbed higher the snow became deeper and more difficult to walk in. It was late and both men were greatly fatigued. A German on skis passed them and asked why they did not have any skis to which they gave the lame excuse that they had not expected the weather!

After a long walk of about ten miles they entered the village of Grunneshubel and mingled with a crowd of villagers. Although they all spoke Czech they were very suspicious and none of them seemed helpful. Then they found a man on his own and confided to him that they were POWs. He nearly had a fit and wanted to run away but they persuaded him not to and he led them up to the Czech border. A few hundred metres before the border he showed them where to leave the road and under the cover of thick woodland they quietly crossed with no trouble. The border was a small stream about two metres wide which they jumped across and joined the road again, safely in Czechoslovakia. There was a small village nearby and they made their way to it. Freddie was now in his home country and felt great relief and more confident but both men were bone weary. They had been walking for many hours in very rough country and their clothes and shoes were thin and flimsy and had not kept out the cold. They were wet to the skin and freezing. If they did not keep on the move they would freeze to death. Both men felt that they could just drop to the ground and fall asleep. They were in bad shape and rapidly losing strength.

On reaching the village of Novi Hradek they entered an inn occupied by parties of skiers who had come up for the weekend. The atmosphere was warm and jovial. They were all so busy drinking that no one seemed to notice them which was surprising as they were soaked to the skin and their clothes looked out of place with the holiday fashions. Taking a great risk Freddie went straight up to the manageress at the reception and told her that they were both escaped prisoners. She responded calmly, showing no sign of surprise, and called her father, the manager, who took them into another room where they sat in front of a large cast-iron stove and warmed up. In half an hour they began to thaw out and with food and drink they felt better. The manager was quite willing to help even though they were complete strangers. Somehow he sensed their great need. The rest of the guests were heavily into gambling and getting drunk and ignored the two strangers despite their appearance. They looked like a couple of escaped convicts! The manager proposed that they should stay in the only unoccupied room left in the hotel. It had a large double bed and after a hot bath they collapsed side by side and slept like babes. The two men, on the run for their freedom and their lives, slept in the lap of luxury for the first time in years. It was so different from the prison camp. The bed was comfortable and warm and the hotel was full of people for whom the war meant so little. It seemed as if they were on another planet.

They stayed at the hotel for several days, regained their strength and made plans to go on to Prague where Freddie had a contact, a barber who had helped other POWs. They also had another contact, Joanne, who was manager of a roadhouse restaurant and was willing to assist escaped prisoners.

The whole of Germany and Czechoslovakia now knew about the escape. Strict checks were conducted by the Germans on all trains and so it was impossible to go on. At that stage nobody knew just how many prisoners had got out but the German Gestapo had been alerted on Hitler's instructions and a tremendous effort was being made to find the escapers. The escape of so many men had thoroughly disrupted the German war resources as it diverted a German SS Panzer Division, thousands of troops and officials, and indirectly many other Germans in various corps. Hitler declared a *Kriegsfahndung* meaning a national manhunt involving the whole country. He had demanded that when captured at least fifty prisoners should be immediately shot.

There was a very real danger of being reported by Czechs who were German sympathisers. The two escapers were hamstrung and could not move until things quietened down. On Tuesday the 28th they left the hotel because of a growing concern that they were about to be raided. The hotel manager arranged for them to move to a barn about ten kilometres away and they left under cover of darkness. They arrived at the barn at 10.00 pm and made a bed in the straw but it was cold and after the luxurious hotel they slept badly. The following day the owner of the barn entered and warned that there were patrols in the vicinity searching for them and they must not leave the barn on any account. Many people had been arrested by the Nazis because their papers were not in order. The Germans were out in full force.

Being holed up in the barn was unbearable for them. They constantly checked to see if any one was approaching. A sound drew their attention.

'Hush,' whispered Des and peered out through a slot in the window.

A cart drew up and an old man opened the double doors and led the horse into the barn. The two POWs dived for cover under the heaps of hay. Grasping a long sharp fork he began to load hay into the cart. Each thrust of the fork came dangerously closer and closer to where they lay. At last Freddie cried out to save themselves and the two men sprang up like jack-in-the-boxes, scattering hay in all directions.

The man got a terrible shock and thrust out the hay fork in a defensive stance.

'You must help us, we are POWs,' they exclaimed.

In dazed fright the man immediately threatened to report them and turned to run. With the speed of desperation Freddie leapt forward, grabbed the man in a vice like grip and disarmed him. In a determined tone he warned him in Czech.

'If that is your attitude, we will kill you here and now,' he breathed into his ear as the man struggled.

The Czech population had been so intimidated by the Gestapo that few Czechs were able to resist the Nazis and they all lived in fear, not only for themselves but also for their families.

Freddie continued his little talk with the man and it worked wonders. He stopped struggling, listened and began to lose his fear. After a while Freddie released his grip and they now talked for a time, explaining their predicament to him. He agreed to cooperate and left quietly, having promised not to spill the beans.

They spent three nights in the barn and the weather became warmer. At last the police checks were removed on the roads and railways. It was time for them to move and on Friday the 31st they did so under cover of darkness. The farmer showed them the way by going ahead along the path while Des and Freddie followed about fifty metres behind. As they climbed a hill the farmer quietly turned away and allowed the two men to continue uninterrupted to a village called Spik where they proceeded to knock at every door but no one would take them in. Each house had a dog and soon the whole village was in bedlam. The dogs knew that the two men were strangers and refused to keep quiet. At the other end of the village they met a farmer milking his cows and he agreed that they could sleep in his barn on condition they left at 4.00 am in the morning! They collapsed in sleep and he woke them in the morning as agreed but they were so tired they could not muster enough strength to get going and begged for more time. Grudgingly he agreed they could stay till evening.

They had hot soup and bread and after a shave and a wash started out to walk the twenty miles to Nachod. It was a clear night but very cold. After many hours dawn broke just as they approached the station. About two hundred metres from the platform a Czech policeman stopped them and asked for their papers. He explained apologetically that many POWs had escaped and he had to stop everyone. He checked them thoroughly, felt their pockets and opened their cases and as he did so became more and more suspicious. He questioned them, examined their documents and queried why Des had no moustache when his photo showed him with one. Des had shaved it off a day or two before. Then he wanted to know what work they did. They replied that they were technicians. Where were their tools? Freddie explained that they were searching for spares. The policeman looked at them and told them their story stank!

Des and Freddie held their breath and waited to see what would happen. To their amazement he told them to get going and turned his back and walked away!

Without waiting to see if he would change his mind they hurried to the station and caught the slow train to Pardubitz which stopped at all stations. They had a few hours to spare in Pardubitz and Freddie thought it a good idea to look up his old landlady with whom he had boarded during his Air Force training in the town. Her flat was just across the road from the Gestapo HQ. The meeting was brief. When she saw him she nearly passed out with shock. She told them of the terrible treatment she had suffered after Freddie had escaped from the Nazi occupation. He had got to Britain and joined the RAF but the Gestapo had grilled her severely and she was now very fearful. They left in a hurry and returned to the station restaurant where they had some watery soup and some coffee. Sitting a few tables away was Freddie's ex training instructor whom he had not seen for some ten years and who now peered at Freddie very closely as if he recognised him. It was a tense moment and the two men finished their meal in haste and left.

They caught a slow train to Prague where they sought out the barber but his shop was closed. Near by was the eating house to which they had been pointed. It too was closed so the two men went around to the back entrance where they found some stairs leading to the first floor but were puzzled to find some large Alsatian dogs guarding the place. They seemed harmless enough so they stepped past them and entered to find a group of Luftwaffe orderlies standing around. A number of men eyed them curiously. They had unwittingly walked right into an emergency hospital attached to the nearby military airport where injured German Air Force personnel were cared for. They smiled stupidly and backed out, patting the guard dogs as they left.

Now they were at a loss as to what to do. They had nowhere to go and spent a sleepless night hiding in a quiet back street. The following day they caught a train to Kolina, a small town near Prague. As they disembarked a plain clothes policeman stopped Des and asked for his identity card. When Des gave it to him he removed it from its plastic covered folder and examined it on both sides with great care. It was so well printed that he could find no fault with it. The forgery department had done a perfect job! He handed it back and Des scooted off. Freddie was waiting in trepidation and complained about his unkempt appearance which drew attention. At midday they returned to Prague and approached the barber's shop. He had returned; they introduced themselves and he was delighted to meet them. First he gave them a great shave and trim. Then he passed on some food coupons and advised them how they could book into an inexpensive hotel and spend a night in comfort before the police checked on their documents. Des and Freddie thought this was a brilliant idea and were soon enjoying a good bed and plenty of food again. They spent three nights moving from hotel to hotel and enjoying the good life before making contact with the manager of the roadhouse. He proved helpful and invited them in.

Des and Freddie talked at great length about their plans and they decided to head for Bregenz on the east end of Lake Constance which bordered Switzerland, Germany and Austria. Early on Friday 7th April they caught a train to Tabor and Pisek. The journey was comfortable and passed through beautiful scenery which reminded Des of England and home. His mind began to drift. So far they had evaded capture and within a short while would be on the last leg of the journey to Switzerland. The thought of home and family brought great comfort. As they travelled along everything seemed far removed from the harsh realities of the war. Tabor was a delightful town in a fairyland. Des had never seen such beautiful architecture ever before, except in picture books. The towers had cone shaped roofs, the streets were spotless and the sky above was clear blue. It was so picturesque Des could hardly believe his eyes. Surely it could not be real! He must be dreaming. They stopped and had an excellent meal.

Good Friday

By evening they had arrived at the delightful little town of Domazlitze nestling in the evening light. It was Good Friday and the Cathedral was dimly lit from the inside with sacred light shining through the colours of the stained glass windows. Holy music came from the interior and Des felt it beckon to them.

'Come inside and worship. The Lord is here,' it seemed to say.

The scene left a lasting impression on Des's mind. Domazlitze was where Huss, the great reformer, had done much of his work and was the centre for some of the great Christian revivals of long ago. Des knew he could not enter the cathedral but he longed to do so. The sense of God's love could not be suppressed even in occupied Europe and he lingered near the building, receiving comfort as he thought about Easter. God was so near.

That night they booked in at a small hotel. The room was cosy and they went down for supper. They handed in their identity documents at the reception as was the custom in all the hotels but to their consternation observed the manager's son scrutinizing the documents with extreme concentration. He showed an unusual interest in them and the two escapers suspected that he was suspicious. Des and Freddie lost their composure and were most disturbed and returned to their room to discuss their fears. The two men disagreed. Freddie was unwilling to remain in the town for any period whereas Des suggested that they should just lie low for a while.

To add to the tension Des had another close call when he went off to the toilet and by accident knocked over a German soldier. The light in the passage had blown and Des was feeling his way in the pitch dark when he collided with the man. They fell sprawling over one another. The German apologised most profusely saying it was all his fault. Des insisted it was really he who was to blame. They dusted one another off and parted the best of friends but it caused some tension between the two escapers who were both on edge. Going to the toilet had become a hazardous exercise! Freddie said Des should be more careful. Once again they were getting on each other's nerves. It was past midnight before they eventually fell into a fitful sleep.

Easter Saturday
After a restless night, they arose early and sneaked out, having paid their bill the previous evening, thankful that the manager and his son had not yet surfaced. It was a beautiful day but somehow a sense of foreboding hung upon the men. Freddie was reluctant to spend the day in Domazlitze so they decided to catch the slow train to nearby Klatovy, arriving just before midday.

They had not counted on one thing; it was the Easter holiday with the trains crowded with travellers and there was an increased police presence with several check points. On arrival at Klatovy the men walked towards the platform exit and Freddie got through with no problems but a Czech policeman stopped Des and demanded to see his identity card. Des showed it to him but after looking at it he insisted on Des producing a travel permit, which he did. The policeman pointed out that the travel permit had expired. Freddie lingered among the crowd but saw that Des was in trouble and in an act of outstanding selflessness returned despite the likelihood of being arrested. Freddie tried to explain that they had only come to Klatovy to see friends. The policeman was not convinced and ordered them to come with him to the local civilian police station to check their identity. He was very pleasant, insisting this was only a formality and still did not suspect they were POWs, but Des knew that their time was up. After all the tension of the past two weeks he nearly fainted with the mental exhaustion but forced himself to try and remain calm. At the police station they were put into a cell where the two men hastily revised their movements to make sure their stories tallied.

An hour later the police returned, their mood drastically changed. Now they had turned nasty. The police were upset, the papers were false, and they were marched off to the Gestapo jail. It was Easter Saturday 1944, the time when many Christians remembered the death and burial of Jesus Christ. The two men were about to walk through their own long, dark valley. Was this to be their tomb – imprisoned in the bowels of a Nazi jail? Could they hope for a resurrection out of this Gestapo hades? Were they to perish under the Kugel Order? With the overwhelming disappointment of capture and the almost certain expectation of execution the two men felt finished. Their prospects looked grim.

CHAPTER 5

Into the Gates of Hell –
Gestapo Custody

'Have you seen the gates of death?'

The Gestapo or *Geheime Staatspolizei* which meant the 'Secret State Police' were greatly feared in occupied Europe. They were a law unto themselves and reported directly to Nazi top man Heinrich Himmler. There was no limit to the methods that they would use to extract information from suspects and the extent of their cruelty was widely experienced. Few people would risk being caught by them and few were able to withstand their torture. Des was to discover firsthand some of their techniques. The worst had now happened – they were in the hands of the Gestapo. What lay ahead? It was with trepidation that the two men contemplated their future. Klatovy Gestapo Gaol was mild compared to the one in Prague but that was still to come. The Gestapo still did not know who Des and Freddie were and they carefully guarded them. They were brought into an office and a gigantic man accompanied by his subordinates entered and began to shout. He was evidently quite angry and the real showdown had not started.

Des and Freddie told the Gestapo that they were escaped POWs and rattled off their number, name and rank. The huge Gestapo man refused to believe this and became even more irate at the apparent lack of respect. The Germans held to the opinion that the two men were plain clothes commandos who

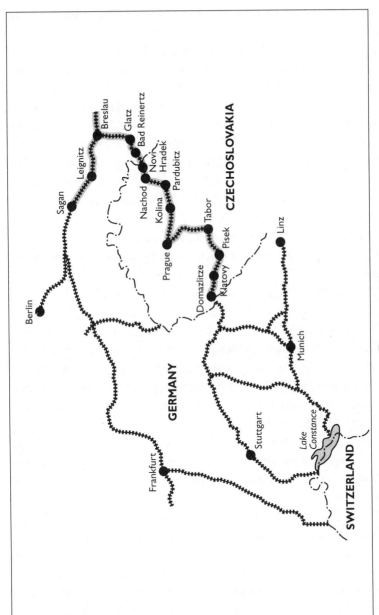

Escape route.

had parachuted into Czechoslovakia to commit sabotage. This was very serious for Des and Freddie because Hitler had given express orders that all commandos should be shot immediately with no exceptions. This was contained in the 'Commando Order' issued by Hitler which stated that all commandos, especially those in plain clothes, who had infiltrated or parachuted into German held territory, should be executed on capture. The only reason this could be delayed was for the purpose of interrogation, by torture if necessary, and then the execution had to be carried out within twenty four hours. If the Gestapo suspected Des and Freddie of being commandos their lives were in immediate danger.

The big man began to shout even louder.

Des and Freddie replied once more by giving their number, name and rank.

The Gestapo then demanded to know their birth dates. The men replied again with number, name and rank, adding that under the rules of the Geneva Convention they were not obliged to divulge more. Well, if the big man was angry before, he now became furious. A battle of wills began. He insisted on knowing their birth dates as he said they were required in order to identify the men. The prisoners replied that they would on no account divulge them.

The big man threatened to shoot them.

'Go ahead and shoot us,' Des shot back with a sudden boldness, 'because then we will not be able to tell you our birthdays.'

The answer flawed the man for a moment. He was speechless at such insolence. Again he insisted they were commandos.

The more they argued the more the big man swore and cursed. He was wild with rage and threatened that if they did not talk quickly they would get down to serious torture. It did not seem to intimidate the men. The more he tried to screw their birthdays out of them the more stubborn the two men became.

He began to shout, '*Geburtstag, Geburtstag!*' over and over, jumping up and down, all the time getting redder and redder.

Des thought he was about to have a heart attack and that if he did it would be a fitting conclusion to the conversation. The more he screamed the more resistance he met. Des and Freddie seemed to have a single mind and for some inexplicable reason were able to show absolutely no fear of him at all. Perhaps it was because they had nothing to lose, being sure their days were numbered anyway. But they saw they were getting the better of the man and he was rapidly losing face. Des enjoyed baiting him and relished the unexpected moral victory won over him.

After a while the Gestapo men cooled down and began to fill in forms. When they came to the date of birth they asked if the dates on the forged identity cards were correct. Des said that perhaps they were but on the other hand perhaps they were not and that was all he could say, they were not prepared to give any further information until they were provided with a proper interpreter – that was only fair as they wanted no further misunderstandings! Everything so far had been conducted in German. The Gestapo eventually copied the forged dates down. The Germans were meticulous for detail and so they put down the dates as better than nothing. They still did not believe that the two men were POWs but that they were parachutists who had dropped into Czechoslovakia. However, their brave front had disarmed the interrogators who did not know what to do with them. There were no interpreters in Klatovy and so they had to take them to Prague and it was probably this delay that saved them from being shot immediately.

Lengthy interrogations followed but fortunately the Nazis had made the bad mistake of leaving the two men together for a couple of days during which time they went over every detail of their story to cover up their tracks and protect all those who had helped them. Nevertheless the pressure that would be brought on the men was so intense that it left psychological scars for years to come. Freddie had been in the hands of the Gestapo once before. Without his advice Des would soon have succumbed but Freddie was meticulous in all his plans and could foresee what the Gestapo would ask. They revised and consolidated their story again and again. There had been numerous people who had risked their lives to help them. If the Nazis found out about any of them they would be killed and probably their families too. They also had to cover for their fellow prisoners and all those who had assisted in the tunnel. It would be very difficult not to make a slip under interrogation. Freddie was very thorough. He had even taught Des how to eat with a knife and fork in the way that the Czechs and Germans did as well as other small points that others might overlook. It is often the little things that give one away, he said. When the Gestapo separated the men and took them away for interrogation the last thing Freddie said to Des was, 'Whatever you do, stick to the story, don't change it for anything.'

They had rehearsed their story so many times and had so discussed every little flaw that in fact the Gestapo had great difficulty finding fault with it! The two men were grilled relentlessly for long periods. The story stood up so well that the Nazis seemed convinced that it was basically true and try as they would could find no loose threads in it. Des and Freddie were able to explain away how they had stayed in hotels and got food without implicating anyone. Physical force was used from time to time by the guards who severely beat up Des on a couple of occasions but the Gestapo preferred to use psychological methods to break the men. The outstanding thing is that they both managed to withstand it and not crack. Des had begun to learn how to handle the guards and escape further beatings. German discipline was always very strict and it was forbidden for any lower rank to touch or disobey an officer of higher rank. When threatened Des would react very strongly and fearlessly screamed at them that he was a British officer.

'Ich bin ein britischer Offizier.'

The word officer had a magical effect. They responded by coming to attention and saluting. The Gestapo were not so easy. Des knew they had the power of life and death and since he knew about the Kugel Order, Des fully expected to be shot – it was simply a matter of time.

The Roasting House

The Gestapo, however, were desperate to know more about the escape. It had caused a major upset in Germany and within the Nazi hierarchy. Two Gestapo men escorted Des and Freddie from Klatovy to Prague. It was a bright spring morning, crisp and fresh, and the men were handcuffed in an open car and had a grand view as they were driven in style through the countryside like visiting dignitaries. They caused a great stir as they passed through the villages and extra precautions were taken by the Gestapo everywhere they went. Des felt very important and imagined himself as a famous war hero waving to crowds of wellwishers. When at last they arrived at Gestapo HQ all the corridors were first cleared before the men were led into the main hall. The Gestapo were determined that they should have no contacts whatsoever with any outsiders.

About twenty five prisoners were sitting in the hall and they were commanded not even to look at the newcomers but to sit absolutely still and bolt upright with their hands on their knees. If anyone moved they were cuffed across the head and if they fell down they were cuffed again and again. The HQ was nicknamed 'The Roasting House' and there was an atmosphere of intense fear prevailing in the place. When Des was brought in, handcuffed and helpless, he soon stopped dreaming as he sensed immediately the sinister fear in the place. Forced to stand against a wall, he endured it for an hour without moving, but then, plucking up courage, Des asked to go to the toilet!

Pandemonium broke out among the guards. After a heated discussion one of them eventually escorted Des down the passage to the toilet. This gave Des a great thrill as he found himself walking on Axminster carpets. The urinals had been made in Stoke-on-Trent which was his wife's home town and the thought seemed to comfort Des. The association of ideas uplifted him as he realised that even in the heart of the Gestapo stronghold there was a little bit of England. He was reminded of the good times he had spent with his wife. How he longed to be with her. He thought of his family and these cherished memories helped strengthen him to face whatever might come his way. He said a silent prayer. After a long time Des's name was called out, 'Ploonkit.'

Pandemonium broke out as guards jumped and the passage was cleared. He and Freddie were thrown into the back of a van and taken to Pankratz Gaol which was infamous during the war for its awful conditions. It was here that Des learnt to speak perfect Czech from a fellow inmate who had a Prague accent. Later, when asked by Czechs where he learnt to speak so well, Des would reply 'In Pankratz.' He need say no more – they all knew what that meant!

After another long wait standing against a wall they were searched and all personal items confiscated. Des and Freddie were separated and although both were miraculously to survive Des and Freddie were never to meet again. Freddie Dvorak was eventually sent to Colditz in Silesia in Germany. Des was thrown into cell 206.

Later two men were placed with Des in his cell who both

spoke perfect English and claimed to be British soldiers. Des had been warned to trust no one whom he did not know but he had not spoken English for so long that it was a delight to do so and he began to relate the full story of their escape to the men – but he gave them the trumped up version just as he told the Gestapo. If these men were plants then they would hear the same story and in the meantime Des was rehearsing it one more time. He was surprised that he could relate it all so easily and without difficulty. This was important as he would again be questioned by the Gestapo. It seemed to Des that the two men were on good terms with the Germans and were asking him questions to satisfy them. They only spent a few days in the cell and were soon removed. On reflection Des felt strongly that they had been planted in the cell to spy on him and was thankful that he had not told them the true story but cursed his folly for sharing with them details about his family as well as other information. He had implied to them that he could get information back to England through a secret code that he used with his brother, Gillian, who was also in the RAF. Des did indeed get news out in this manner as he and his brother had worked out a simple code that could be used in such an event but the prospect of having compromised himself became a nightmare.

On 11th May a young Czech man of about twenty years of age was placed in cell 206. He had been accused of sabotage. The Gestapo made every effort not to mix civilians with prisoners of war and the fact that they had done so convinced Des that his own fate had already been sealed. He became more and more sure that they would liquidate him because he was one of the top men involved with the production of maps and other false papers used in the escape. On the 26th two British Army officers were placed in the cell and the young man taken out. It was a great relief for Des. To Des's amazement one of the

men personally knew his uncle who was a solicitor in
Edinburgh so Des knew that they were genuine. They had been
caught in North Africa and then moved to Europe. They
remained with Des for a few weeks but once again he was
careful not to divulge too much. However, one of them, Tommy
Wedderburn, did manage to get a coded letter back to Des's
wife saying that he was alive in a Gestapo jail. Des's brother,
mother and wife took the letter to the Air Ministry to discuss it
with them. His brother met with Group Captain Walker who
had worked with Des in the past. The officer gave strict
instructions to the family not to divulge the contents of the
letter to anyone else as it could have serious repercussions for
Des who could even be shot if the Gestapo knew he had got a
message out.

When Des was placed back into solitary confinement he
began to live just one day at a time. While on his own he had
time to think on the whole situation and how miraculous it was
that he was still alive when so many odds were against him. At
this stage he did not know how many other prisoners had
survived nor the awful truth about the execution of his fifty
friends and fellow officers of Stalag Luft III. He thought about
the many people who gave them help and hospitality while on
the run and the bonds of friendship that had been knit in the
midst of adversity and danger. He recalled the days of his youth
and especially the UPSC 'Universities and Public Schools Camp'
near Barmouth in Wales when he had first committed his life to
God and Jesus Christ. He remembered the long discussions he
had had with his youth instructor on the Bible, God and Jesus.
Could it be that God was with him even now in this cell? He
wondered what the future held. He was fortunate to have a
small New Testament left with him by Tommy which he read
constantly. It was printed by the Gideons, an international group
that distributed Bibles to needy people. It gave him strength and

hope but surrounded by so much suffering he could not fully understand the passages that described the love of God. Nevertheless, he literally clung to the New Testament even though it was forbidden for him to have it. One day a Gestapo officer unexpectedly entered the cell and caught Des reading it. The officer snatched the book away but Des clutched it back. A battle of wits began but Des valued the book far too much to let it go.

'What are you doing with this? Give it to me,' came the command.

Des had an unusual boldness and stood his ground.

'This is doing me no harm – everyone here should read it,' he retorted.

The two men glared at each other, their eyes and wills locked together over the battered little book, and then the officer let go, wheeled around and left the cell.

The main interrogation that Des endured was very interesting, to put it mildly. The Gestapo had to find out more about the escape and how it was engineered. They said that if Des told them all they wanted to know they in turn would tell him some very good news at the end. The first session lasted all day. They questioned Des tirelessly on everything to do with the planning of the escape: who made the maps, the permits, the identity cards and the compasses. Des told them again and again that he did not know because they were simply handed out to all the prisoners. Having grilled him on this they started on the escape and wanted to know who had helped them. Once more Des went through his carefully rehearsed story and stuck to it despite the relentless pressure. At last, at the end of the day, the Gestapo said that they would now tell Des the good news.

'The City of London,' they said, 'has been reduced to a heap of rubble through Germany's new secret weapon.'

Des feigned mock horror at the news and the Gestapo were

most pleased with his apparent distress. Des had heard about the V-1 rockets but did not know how effective they had been. They were first launched against Britain on 13th June 1944 and the last one came over on 29th March 1945. Of the total 6,725 that were known to have been launched, 3,935 were destroyed. Of these 1,859 were knocked out by anti-aircraft guns, 1,846 by the RAF and 230 by barrage balloons. However, 2,790 flying bombs got through – killing 15,500 people, injuring 18,000 others and destroying 23,000 homes.

The Führer's Fury
Unknown to Des, all the others, save the three that had got home, had now been rounded up. On the instructions of Hitler who was furious that so many had escaped and was determined to take vengeance upon them, forty seven of them had already been executed. Earlier in 1944 Hitler had issued the infamous 'Kugel Order' (the Bullet Order) which said that all escaping prisoners should be shot on capture. At the news of the mass break-out he went into one of his demonic rages and demanded that all the prisoners should be shot as soon as captured. Hermann Goering, who was in charge of the Luftwaffe and all air prisoners, had objected, saying that to kill them all would not look good. Hitler then modified his order but still insisted that at least fifty should be killed. Des and Freddie Dvorak were the last prisoners to be caught and together with Des's good friend Ivo Tonder were likely to be the next three to be shot to complete the number fifty. However, their execution was delayed. The Gestapo were keen to interview them as they suspected a link to a possible internal uprising in Czechoslovakia. This saved Des from death and because of this the three men escaped being murdered on the orders of Hitler. Later, at the Nuremburg trials, Goering testified that Hitler considered the breakout by the airmen to be a very serious incident. Out of the seventy six men

who got out of Sagan only three made it home. Fifty were shot on the express orders of Hitler and only twenty three survived as prisoners again. Of these, eight were held by the Gestapo for further interrogation.

Hitler's Hit List

General A. Nebe who was head of the Kripo (the German Civilian Police) was selected by Heinrich Himmler, in overall charge of the Gestapo, to have the unenviable task of selecting the names of those to be shot. All fifty were to be shot by the Gestapo on the pretence of trying to escape. In fact most of them were shot on lonely roads in the back of the head while relieving themselves. They were then immediately cremated and their ashes returned to Sagan in urns. At Nuremburg, General Alfred Jodl, Chief of Operations of the Armed Forces High Command during the war, described the killing of the fifty airmen as 'sheer murder'. It was a blatant disregard for the Geneva Convention and as such came under the category of a war crime. Hitler had adopted a deliberate policy of brutality towards all captured airmen after the Allies increased their bombing of Germany from 1943. In the early part of the war Allied airmen who had been shot down in German-held territory were usually treated with respect and even kindness. However, later the policy was to kill all Allied airmen who bailed out and were captured. Civilians were encouraged to lynch the flyers as soon as they had parachuted to the ground and Hitler gave top-secret orders to POW camp commandants to shoot all escapers. When the news of the mass murders leaked out, the British Foreign Minister, Anthony Eden, immediately made an announcement to the House of Commons. He denounced the murders and promised that when the war was over those responsible would be brought to trial.

'Nobody Gets Out of Here Alive'

Des knew nothing of all this.

In Pankratz the Gestapo taunted him with the claim that 'no one ever got out of the jail alive'. Des knew his days were numbered. At Pankratz he mixed with numerous other prisoners, all with their own stories, having fallen foul of the Gestapo in one way or another.

Just down the passage Jan Tonder, brother to Ivo Tonder, occupied a cell. One day soon after Des's arrival in Prague, and during the exercise period, Jan stopped to tie up his shoe-lace and then fell in behind Des. He had heard about Des through the prison grapevine. The two men got talking and Jan told how both his mother and wife were in the same jail but that he did not know what had happened to his brother Ivo. After Ivo's escape they had all been arrested and thrown in jail. The Gestapo had special authority to arrest what were called reprisal prisoners – in other words members of the families of those who were suspected guilty of offences. This practice served as a deterrent for those who would oppose them. Jan spread the word to all the others in the jail that Des was an escaped prisoner of war and from then on many of them helped Des in any way they could. They all had great respect for him.

One day the guards conducted a search on the cells in order to look for knives and other things. During the search the prisoners were taken out to exercise in a square on the other side of the jail. After a strenuous time of forced exercises they were commanded to sit down and allowed to rest. All of a sudden Des heard his name coming out of the nearby wall.

'Plunk, Plunk.' The voice came again. 'Plunk, Plunk.'

Des was puzzled and could not find the source of the voice. He had to be careful not to attract attention so was unable to get up to locate its origin.

'Plunk, Plunk.' It seemed to materialise from out of nowhere.

Was he finally going mad? It was the voice of Ivo Tonder, or his spirit.

Listening carefully Des discovered a small window high in the nearby wall partially open as it hung from the top hinge. Ivo was unable to see through the window but from where he was at the bottom of the cell could make out the reflection of Des on the glass. For a while they shared their news. It was as if a divine hand had planned it all. Des informed Ivo that his brother and family were still alive and he was greatly encouraged. Ivo was later imprisoned at Colditz, Silesia in Germany but Des and Ivo were to meet again in a wonderful way.

A man called Honso was eventually put into cell 206. He was a farmer who only spoke Czech and it was from him that Des learnt how to speak Czech with a Prague accent. Honso saved Des's life for he was allowed food parcels sent from home which he shared with Des. Without them Des felt he would surely have died. Honso was charged with sabotage of the railways but survived imprisonment and the war although he nearly died in a concentration camp before it ended. Soon afterwards another Czech was placed in the cell, a man named Chudoba. He was an untrustworthy character who had spied for the Germans but had fallen foul of them. In fact he had deliberately got himself imprisoned on some minor charge, his reason being to protect himself from the Allies when they eventually defeated the Nazis. He ran with the hare and hunted with the hounds. Within minutes of his arrival the prison grapevine was sending messages warning Des to have nothing to do with him. Des heard after the war that he had been sentenced by the Allies to ten years for crimes he had committed against Allied prisoners during the war.

Yet another man arrived at cell 206 – Alois Laubova. He was totally fearless. During the First World War he had escaped from Hungary and had fought a long hard road back to Czechoslovakia and freedom. Now the Gestapo had arrested him for working in the underground resistance and thrown him into Pankratz awaiting execution. He encouraged Des immensely because he had such a courageous outlook and a great sense of humour. He could speak fluent Russian and was always coming up with anecdotes about the two languages, Russian and Czech. They both belong to the Slavic group of languages but can have marked differences in meaning. One expression that really tickled Des was that a courting couple might say, 'What a lovely life you have.' But in Russian it sounds like, "What a red belly you have.' Alois was always cracking jokes like this. He was found guilty of sabotage and his days were numbered. He told Des that he was due for the guillotine but the prospect did not overwhelm him and he lived each day with great courage. After a while he was taken away and not seen again. It is generally a true observation to say that the righteous have greater strength and fortitude when faced with death than those who are guilty of great wickedness.

Des began to suffer from teeth problems. One wisdom tooth in particular became painful and he plucked up courage and requested that he might see the jail dentist. The prisoners had to pay to go to the dentist and Des was given the required amount by a friend, Horsa Keuma. Despite dreadful tales from those who had gone to the dentist Des determined to put on a brave face. When he entered the room he cheerfully greeted the dentist in Czech. Unfortunately the dentist turned out to be a German with little sympathy for Czechs of any size or shape. He swung into action and merrily drilled away at the roots of the tooth without giving any kind of anaesthetic. Beads of sweat popped out of Des's forehead as he endured the excruciating pain and he began to regret his decision. It seemed the dentist was part of the Gestapo's private torture chamber.

The guillotine was kept in the basement and was busy every

day. It was cheaper than bullets. Prisoners on the first and second floors could hear it operating. They would relay its activity to the rest of the jail.

'Yesterday there were only eleven, but today there were seventeen.'

This information was passed from cell to cell but if they were caught communicating they were in trouble. A Gestapo officer could on any whim take a prisoner out to the courtyard and shoot him. On some days up to eight people were shot. At one time Des began to wish that they would hurry up with his turn and it would all be finished. The daily, even momentary, likelihood of imminent death wore the prisoners down and caused great fear. It was not so much the moment of death that was feared but rather the waiting for it. It required a special fortitude to withstand this psychological pressure and continue to live the daily routine with composure and hope. For much of the time Des was in solitary confinement but he drew strength from the New Testament and also the words of the Psalms which seemed so appropriate for his situation.

On Tuesdays and Thursdays boiled blood from the kitchen was brought around to the cells. This was used to bait the Jewish inmates who, of course, did not choose to eat it. The wardens would also bait the others by saying that the blood came from the basement guillotine. Des never knew whether it was from the kitchen or the guillotine. On some occasions he had such hunger pains that he had to eat something and he could never decide which was worse, the pains from hunger or the distress from eating the blood.

His health was now very bad. He had lost a lot of weight, was physically weak and suffered from depression and despair.

Fortunately, when Honso joined his cell food became more abundant. Not only did Honso get food parcels but on the suggestion of a sympathetic warden he wrote to his family and asked if they could increase the supply. Every two weeks a 20kg parcel would arrive for him. The warden would then throw it into the cell, loudly protesting that he would have to confiscate everything.

As he threw each item in he would declare loudly, 'This is forbidden,' or, 'This is not allowed,' or, 'I will take this away.'

It was a beautiful sham and worked well and cell 206 began to eat again. The problem now was where to hide the food but without it Des knew he would surely have died.

On the morning of 6th June a strange silence fell over the jail. As the Czech wardens were handing out the daily ration of bread and chicory they came to each door and whispered:

'*Invasia.*'

Instead of the usual screams, commands and curses the Gestapo had strangely lost their voice. It was a day Des never forgot. The silence was such a contrast to the normal abuse and the whole jail was filled with an electrifying tension. Everyone knew that the invasion had begun and Hitler's days were now numbered. The subdued silence lasted about two weeks. The whole jail seemed to have turned into a Trappist monastery with people sitting in their cells praying or quietly contemplating the future. Every Nazi seemed to be in a deep state of shock with an air of hopelessness. Hitler had said that German territory could never be invaded and they all knew it was the beginning of the end.

However, the end of the conflict was still some way off and for some would never come in time. More months passed in a dreadful routine that seemed like hell itself. Des clutched at any news that filtered through of victories and advancing troops. It gave him the strength not to give up.

The constant waiting had been hard on all the prisoners. Month after month they clung to the hope that the promised invasion would be rapid and yet the prospect of rescue still seemed so far off. Uppermost in their thinking was the question, 'Would they make it in time?'

On the morning of 10th December Des was on exercise in the yard when an imprisoned Austrian general fell in behind him. Des had got to know him very well. He was General Petre, a man who had been in charge of supplies for the German army on the southern front of the Russian campaign. He had been arrested on suspicion of embezzling funds.

He whispered in German, 'How long will the war go on?'

Des replied, 'Another three months or so.'

'What a pity,' he replied, 'tomorrow I am going to be executed.'

Des did not know what to say but that very day, soon after the exercises were over, Des was taken from his cell and transferred to Hradin prison which was on top of a hill in Prague.

He felt it was a reprieve and that he had made it through the gates of hell. Against all odds he had survived. That any of the POWs should have been spared was remarkable considering Hitler's orders, and then to survive the Gestapo incarceration was almost miraculous. The Gestapo were a law unto themselves and thousands of people who went through their hands simply disappeared. Des was held in Gestapo custody from 4th May to 10th December, most of it at Pankratz Jail in Prague under terrible conditions. His life hung in the balance during that entire period and at any moment he could have been taken out and shot. He was now totally debilitated and physically and mentally finished.

An escort was provided to transfer Des to Hradin Jail which was full of German deserters. The escort was one of the very first men who had interrogated him. This Gestapo officer commented to Des how lucky he was to be alive. Apparently he thought all prisoners should have been shot and told Des so! He also told Des that his name had ranked ninth on a list compiled by top Nazi officials of all those who had escaped and circulated to all Gestapo units with the express orders from Hitler himself that all on the list were to be immediately executed. Des did not stop to think about it but shrugged it off as nonchalantly as he could and took the chance to tell the officer that Germany was finished and would soon be defeated. Of the twenty three prisoners that were not murdered fifteen were soon returned to Sagan but the remaining eight were kept by the Gestapo for 'special treatment' which usually meant death. Ivo Tonder had been one of these and was only spared because he was a Czech. All the others captured and held with Ivo were shot. The Gestapo had suspected an orchestrated plan within Czechoslovakia to disrupt the war effort and had wanted to find out more about it and so held onto Ivo because he was a Czech, suspecting that he was involved in it. This may have been why Des and Freddie were also held in Gestapo custody for so long. Des and Freddie were the last to be caught and this undoubtedly saved them from death. If they had been caught earlier there is little doubt that Des would have been shot because of his status as one of the leaders of the escape. Freddie was a Czech but Des was not and yet for some reason he had been spared.

Of the eight men retained by the Gestapo four of them actually dug their way out of another top security Gestapo jail and made yet another bid for freedom!

The four men – Wings Day, Jimmy James, Johnny Dodge and Sydney Dowse, together with another man, Jack Churchill – dug out of a cell in the Gestapo Sachsenhausen concentration camp. On arrival they had been informed by the Gestapo staff that there was no possible way of escape but undeterred, the five men started a tunnel under the bed and made another dramatic getaway. They all got out but were eventually recaptured and placed in death cells awaiting execution which never came about. In fact something quite extraordinary happened. One day Johnny Dodge was dragged from his cell, given a wash and a shave and clean civilian clothing and transported by luxury car to Berlin where he met with a high ranking official and was informed that he was about to be sent back home! Having fully expecting to be executed he could not believe what was happening. His many attempts at escape were legendary and he had suffered terrible reprisals by the Gestapo. Now he was being sent home at their expense! He could hardly believe it but it transpired that he had been selected to carry a message back to Winston Churchill to the effect that the Reich was wanting to make peace. Johnny was a relative of Churchill's through the American side of the family and the Germans felt he would have some influence on the British leader. Johnny was more than happy to be a messenger boy. Shortly afterwards he was released at the Swiss border and made his way back to Britain where he actually had dinner with Churchill but by then it was too late to talk peace – the war was nearly over and the German Reich about to surrender. The other men also eventually got back. As the war drew to an end there was a lot of confusion among the retreating Germans and many prisoners were moved from place to place. The three men took the opportunity during a forced march to make yet another bid for freedom. They dropped out of the column and managed to get through enemy lines and into Italy where they were rescued by advancing Americans.

CHAPTER 6

Hradin Jail

*'For the Lord looked down, to hear the groaning of the
prisoners, to set free those that are doomed to death.'*

If Des had thought the Gestapo accommodation was uncomfortable he was about to get a rude awakening at Hradcin. He had survived the Gestapo but more was to come. On arrival he was thrown into an empty cell but soon found he was not the only occupant – it was swarming with lice! He spent his time continually squashing them but they just kept coming. Des had had no problems with lice in previous jails as despite everything else the Gestapo were scrupulously clean about their accommodation.

When he explored his cell he looked into the cast iron stove which was set in the middle of the floor and to his surprise found what looked like the fur lining of Freddie Dvorak's coat collar. The discovery deeply affected Des, who had not seen Freddie since a few days after their capture, and his mind snapped. He became demented, hammering on the door in a frenzy, raving in a deranged state of mind, and shouting incoherently. When the guard came Des waved the collar under his nose, screaming all the time, 'What have you done with Freddie?'

The guard went off but soon returned with some others who violently manhandled Des into another cell which was the smallest one he had ever been in. It was about one and a half

76

metres long and so low as to prohibit him standing upright. He occupied this cell, together with the lice, for the rest of his stay. There were many deserters in the jail and they were constantly being shot, which did not provide him with a sense of security. The Nazis executed more than 30,000 of their own troops for desertion and other offences during the war.

The food was meagre and Des lost more weight. He noticed that sometimes potato peelings were thrown into the dustbins at the end of the passage of the cell block and at times he was allowed down the passage to get water. He began to plan his water trips to coincide with the discarding of the potato peel. He was thin and weak and it took him great effort to make his way, swaying precariously, to the dustbins. Whenever he could he grabbed a handful. These were delicious and helped to ward off his hunger.

To keep his mind busy he managed to get some paper and a pencil from a guard and he began to develop projects that he would work on after the war. It kept his mind occupied although it was hard to concentrate. He went back to his original profession of designing and drawing. Des was an expert draughtsman and a good artist. He had various schemes in mind. One was an aero-engine with a new cooling system. Another was a single seater racing aircraft. He dreamt of what he would do after the war with all his inventions and it helped relieve the tension and boredom of prison routine and to create a sense of hope for the future. It also took his mind off the constant stench of the toilet bucket. He began to live in a dream world totally disorientated from the harsh reality around him.

Christmas 1944

Des spent Christmas 1944 in the jail and the chief warden provided him with a Christmas meal. This was not much better than usual but it was a gesture Des would not forget. It was not a very happy Christmas but when New Year came some of the wardens wished him a Happy New Year! There was a changed attitude among the staff. Some of the officials knew that the war would soon be over and sympathised with the Allies. There were good men amongst them and Des had got to know some of them quite well. All of them, staff and prisoners, longed for the war to end.

And then, just as Des was getting to the end of his resources the miracle happened. On 25th January Des left the jail behind. He was suddenly called from his tiny cell and escorted by two Luftwaffe men to the POW camp called Stalag Luft I near Barth in North Germany. It was like the resurrection! He was lifted out of the lowest circumstances of his life. Those seven weeks had nearly killed him. The cell had become a tomb and he was like a living corpse clinging to an existence in living hell. Now it seemed to him as though a giant hand had reached down and plucked him out of the tomb. With his release came a new strength of life in his body.

For Des the journey was filled with wonders. He could hardly dare to believe it was happening. The two Luftwaffe men appeared to Des as angels of mercy to rescue him, old friends, whom he welcomed with deep gratitude. They travelled on a train transporting German Luftwaffe and Des engaged them in conversation. It seemed they had all been reduced to the same level and now, no longer as captors or prisoners, victors or vanquished, were able to speak to one another as men sharing the same hopes and fears. Des asked about the progress of the war and its ultimate end. They told him of the bombing of England but agreed with him that it could never succeed and the only way to defeat Britain was to occupy the land. Des expressed his conviction that Germany could not win and that Hitler was their greatest enemy.

One man asked him, 'Why are you British fighting the Germans when your real enemy is Russia?'

Des replied by turning the question. 'Can you not see that your real enemy is Hitler?' he asked. 'In his book *Mein Kampf* he said the only way to fight and win a war was to fight the enemy one by one but today he has taken on the whole world which means he must be a *Dumkopf*!'

They all agreed except one SS officer scowling in the corner who protested for some time against Des but with no support from the others. Times were changing, thought Des. Another man who had just returned from the Russian front told Des about the overwhelming odds there.

'When one Russian is shot, three stand up,' he related, shaking his head. It reminded Des of his lice.

Des saw wounded men coming back from the front. One wounded SS officer asked the escorting Luftwaffe officers to let him speak to Des alone in the corridor. He wanted to confess to Des his burden of guilt and his fears for the future. He had been forced to enlist in the SS on threat of reprisals against his family who would have lost everything they had, their homes and business and even their lives. The man had seen and participated in horrific deeds. He poured out confessions of guilt to Des and asked for understanding and forgiveness for the things he and his nation had done. Des tried to give the man some comfort: the war would soon be over, he said, and then everyone could go back to being normal again – if that was truly possible. There was evidently a marked change of attitude among many of them who had now lost their bravado and, facing defeat, realised that Hitler was to blame for the destruction of the nation. When Des was transferred onto another train a small group of Nazis began to insult him. They taunted him because he looked so pitifully weak and thin, as well as mocking a young Jewish girl who was being escorted under arrest. One man, however, interjected and encouraged Des not to listen. 'They are not the true Germans,' he said.

A Prisoner in Despair

Des arrived at Stalag Luft I on 27th January 1945, ten months after the tunnel escape. He was physically and emotionally exhausted by the harrowing experience. The tactics used by the Gestapo were deliberately geared to wear people down and eventually caused many of them to take their own lives. Des was a shell of a man but he had somehow clung to his faith that God was looking after him. Now he was to face the greatest test of all. As he went through the usual procedure of having his photo taken and his particulars recorded, Des learnt for the first time about the death of many of his colleagues. The shocking news had a profound and disturbing effect on him and sent him into a deep trauma. The months of suffering had taken a severe toll upon his health and mental state and he had no reserves left. He was deeply scarred. Now a sense of guilt descended upon Des such as he had never known before. The more he thought about the frightful news the more he blamed himself for it. He was convinced that he had contributed to the deaths of his colleagues by somehow incriminating them during his interrogation. The guilt that possessed Des was not visible or tangible and was an insidious thing that destroyed him from the inside. At Stalag Luft I he had a complete collapse. The tension of the escape, the weeks on the run followed by capture, and the interrogations, the harsh conditions, the constant confinement and the daily threat of death had devastated him. Now the heavy weight of self inflicted guilt gnawed at his resolve.

Yet another problem beset Des. He was now also suspected of being a Nazi sympathiser and was not accepted by the other prisoners. He was considered a German plant. Many of the prisoners were Americans and had been captured fairly recently. They had no understanding of what Des had been through. None of them knew him and they were sure he was a spy. One American Major who was in charge of the block publicly rebuked Des and from then on the POWs deliberately ostracised him. Des had borrowed some cigarettes from a German guard and when he later came to return them he was seen by the Major. It was a common practice at Sagan to borrow cigarettes from the guards but Des did not know that it was not allowed at Stalag Luft 1. Instead of a quiet correction Des was publicly reprimanded and accused of being a German collaborator and spy. This was too much for him. To have gone through all he had and then to be accused of being a spy broke him completely. Being rejected by his own people so demoralised Des that he had a total mental breakdown and sank into a darkness deeper than anything he had yet encountered. He became a prisoner to guilt and rejection.

Two Canadian officers who knew of him, Squadron Leader Robertson and Group Captain Weir, managed to get him into the camp hospital and tried to reassure him by telling him that most of the executions of the escaped airmen had taken place before he was recaptured so that he had nothing to do with them. They visited him daily but Des remained in dark despair. He constantly contemplated suicide and his mind began to slip until one night at about midnight he got out a razor blade with the intention of slashing his wrists. Then he clearly heard a voice from somewhere speak to him:

'Why are you being a coward, why not face the music?' it said.

The words had a profound effect upon him. Slowly he began to pull through the mental anguish but the spiritual damage lasted many years. Many men who had been through such events were emotionally and spiritually wounded for life. Outwardly they looked normal but inwardly they were in deep turmoil and suffered from insecurity and fear. Some of them were never able to rebuild their lives. Others even took their lives after the war ended. Such is the aftermath and tragedy of war. Des was overcome not so much by the experiences he had endured but rather by a strange sense of guilt. It was not the treatment in the jails that broke him but the awful reality of the death of so many of his personal friends and colleagues. Not only did he blame himself for their deaths but in a strange way he felt guilty that he had been spared when so many of them had perished. This played on his mind and he would not be free of its destructive consequences for over twenty five years.

As Des began to recover, unexpected aid came to his assistance. The camp hospital was just a few metres from the adjacent compound in which many Czechs were imprisoned. Standing at the hospital window Des called in Czech to the passing prisoners as they paraded along the fence. What joy it was for him as he was recognised by old friends from previous prison encounters. Again and again they would greet him, surprise and excitement lighting up their haggard faces. It became a daily routine for the duration of his stay in hospital and of course this was reported to the Senior British Officer. With so many prisoners vouching for him, all suspicions of Des's true identity were erased. When he recovered sufficiently to leave the hospital Des continued to mix with the Czech speaking prisoners. After his long time in Prague jails he spoke Czech perfectly with a Prague accent! One day a British officer commented, 'That red haired Czech speaks good English.' Des took it as a compliment.

Rescue

Des remained a prisoner until the end of April 1945. On 28th April all the German staff at the POW camp mysteriously disappeared. They had got wind of advancing Allied armies and had slipped away from the approaching Russians. There was a quietness over the whole camp as the prisoners waited. On the 29th the Russian army arrived in the vicinity. The POWs had made plans for the time that Germany would surrender and had formed themselves into emergency squads trained in unarmed combat. Des was with a group of twenty men who were ordered to clear the nearby airport of huge 250 kg bombs. The retreating Germans had scattered them over the airfield to prevent the Allies from landing. At first the men were very careful about how they handled the bombs but after a while became quite nonchalant and threw them around without fear. It took them ten days to clear the field to allow the Americans to fly in.

Des was to have one more close shave before he got out of Germany. He was now fluent in Czech and Russian and had been selected by his commanding officer to go out and meet the advancing Russian soldiers as they approached the airfield. He had a pistol and was to fire a red flare if there was trouble or a green one if all was well. Dressed in American uniforms Des and two companions approached the advance party of four Russian soldiers who appeared to be no more than teenagers. The Russians aggressively thrust their guns into Des's stomach and demanded to know who he was. His two companions stayed back about 50 metres so Des was on his own. The Russians grabbed the flare gun out of his hands and fired the first flare straight into the ground, just missing his feet. Des had to keep on repeating that he was an 'Americanetz' until eventually the message sunk in. Then they dropped their guns and gave him the famous bear hug after which they fired off all the flares into the sky. What a great sight it was, like Guy Fawkes! A few days later the advancing Americans arrived and rescue became a reality.

Flight to Freedom

There were over ten thousand prisoners that had to be flown out of Stalag Luft I and the Americans organised it with hardly a hitch. They used thirty five B17 Fortress aircraft and airlifted the men out in batches. It was about 8th May that the airlift started and it continued for three days. The POWs lined up on the tarmac in companies and boarded the planes. One plane was kept stationary on the tarmac with its engines running as a control centre and radio tower. Planes flew in every few minutes. As soon as one was loaded it took off and the next taxied up.

Des was on the last of four aircraft to leave. He had been active right to the end. He had also, in those last few days, seen sights that would remain with him all his life. Many civilians, Jews and others, had suffered and as the advancing Russian troops overran the country there were scenes of violence and tragedy. Many prisoners who came out of concentration camps were starving. Des never forgot the smell of the dead and dying. Near the airport was a POW camp with about 1,500 Russian prisoners and other nationalities who were all in a terrible condition. The British and Americans tried to help where possible.

One day some children were playing about fifty metres away when an explosion rocked the vicinity. Des ran up to find a youngster had triggered a booby trap left by the withdrawing troops. His hand was blown off. After giving first aid Des made a point of taking the child home to his mother who lived nearby. She had already suffered much and her husband had not returned from the Russian front and was unlikely to do so. Des did his best to comfort the woman. At this time many German civilians were devastated as their land was invaded and they were subjected to the occupying forces. The Russians were rolling in, first in their tanks and then in armoured cars, followed by troops and supply vehicles. They had come to stay. They brought a new reign of terror to the civilians who were mostly confused and bewildered. Women were raped and there was a great deal of looting. Des was thankful to see the last of it.

He boarded an aircraft for home but on the way it circled around Hamburg to allow the passengers to see the effect of the Allied bombing. Des was once more profoundly shocked to see that the entire city centre was demolished. As a prisoner he had not heard the full extent of the war's progress. The aircraft crossed the English Channel and Des could not help but recall that fateful evening, now so long ago, that he had flown in the other direction. It was a miracle he was coming back. The impact of his return began to affect him deeply. He was not yet over his traumatic breakdown and half expected to be arrested on arrival for being a Nazi sympathiser: such are the tricks of the mind. He feared rejection from his own people and family. The aircraft landed at Ford Airfield, near Haywards Heath, close to where his mother lived, and it was with mixed feelings of trepidation and relief that he stepped out onto British soil. It was an emotional moment and many wept. The men were taken to a tent and treated to tea and sandwiches. And what a treat it was to see white bread after three years of 'pumpernickel', the German black bread. The ladies that served him spoke pure English – what heaven! Later Des and some others went off to a local pub and tasted good old English beer.

Home, Loved Ones and Reunion

As Des thought about home, wife and daughter he did not know what to expect. He was 50 lbs below his normal weight and had deep emotional scars. Many prisoners of war suffered in ways different from those who were never captured. The restriction of freedom and the often daily fear of death affected some men grievously. Des had never seen his daughter and had not heard from his wife for over a year. She had not even known if he was still alive. As he travelled on the train in the direction of home and reunion with his loved ones his heart was filled with a mixture of joy, elation and uncertainty. He just could not believe that this moment had come at last, after years of dreaming about it. It seemed to him that even the train knew he was on board and he felt that he was a privileged person. He had survived the odds. Perhaps someone bigger than the Gestapo and the war had been looking after him all the time – there could be no other explanation.

His family reunion was sweet. It took place at his mother's home. His wife Patsy looked a dream. Little Maureen was very possessive of her mother. In the morning when she came into the bedroom she was surprised to see a man in bed with her mummy. She jumped into bed and pushed Des out! By the end of the first day Des and she were getting on like old friends. Des was thrilled to get to know her but another surprise just capped it all.

After their arrival his mother said to Des that she had a special present waiting for him upstairs. They went up to the bedroom and Des was overcome with joy to find his brother Nigel, whom he thought to be dead, waiting there to give him a surprise. They fell into each other's arms.

Nigel had also been a POW very early in the war and spent many years behind wire. He had been wounded and then forced to do heavy manual work. He escaped once and was free for nineteen days before recapture. Then towards the end of the war he managed to escape again and this time got back to Britain! In January 1945 he and many other POWs had been forced to march into the interior of Germany to escape the advancing Russians. It had been bitterly cold – many POWs disappeared in the confusion and many died. Nigel had gone

missing and Des had learnt from one of his fellow prisoners that
Nigel had perished.

Here he was standing, alive and well. Des was astounded to
see him and amazed to hear his story. He and an American had
dropped out of the marching column of prisoners and buried
themselves in the snow. They then walked across country until
they came upon some Polish soldiers who helped them. They
stole a cart and a pony and loaded it with supplies but when the
Russian advance caught them in a village the cart and pony
were demolished by the bombardment. They had nothing left
but managed to scrape together some food and carry on,
eventually meeting up with some Poles who got them onto a
slow train to Odessa. The train was crammed full with hundreds
of refugees, all trying to reach some place that was safe. Europe
was in total chaos. Many Russians were on the train and without
exception every Russian they met was collecting watches. They
had them all around both wrists and even on their ankles. Nigel
and his companion sold whatever they had to get provisions
and got to the coast. At Odessa they were fortunate enough to
find a British ship and enjoyed a cruise all the way home, getting
there before Des. What a joyful reunion there was in the
Plunkett home that night.

CHAPTER 7

A New Career

'Behold I make all things new.'

At the end of the war Des found himself among hundreds of other redundant Air Force men who were out of work. He had been debriefed by a Major Randall who spent almost a full day with Des and was amazed that Des had withstood times of solitary confinement in the Gestapo jails and the harsh conditions. At the end of the debrief he simply commented, 'I admire your lone fight against the Nazis.' But Des's fight was not over yet. For years he would know inner conflict that would drive him to near disaster.

Many pilots and officers applied to rejoin the Royal Air Force but only a few were taken in. Des reported for his interview and was told to come back in two weeks at which time he was informed, much to his pleasure, that he was accepted. He remained with the Royal Air Force for another two years. In order to return to general duties he went through several refresher courses and a time of training. After a Conversion course in England at Sywell on Dakota aircraft he was posted to India and joined Ten Squadron, popularly known as the 'Shiny Ten'. The squadron had a long history of service in Burma and Des was pleased to join them. He was occupied with general duties on Dakotas carrying supplies and ferrying passengers all around India. It was at this time that a new design in parachutes was being tested in India and several had malfunctioned

Douglas Bader left, with Peter Casanova and Des on right.

resulting in the deaths of a number of Air Force men. The new parachute had a smaller canopy diameter of 28 feet as opposed to the 35 foot canopy then in use. For some reason the new parachutes formed 'Roman Candles' by not opening properly and twisting around. The experts came out from Britain and corrected the error whereupon the commanding officer asked for volunteers to test them. Des stepped forward and soon found himself and some others bundled into an aircraft to test the chute – the second time he had ever jumped in his life.

The modified parachute performed without a hitch!

Des was in India during the period leading up to independence which were turbulent times and during which there was much violence. He had been rated with top grades for Dakotas and had been asked to become Lord Mountbatten's personal pilot but refused the offer and instead became involved in conducting an aerial survey of the proposed Indian-

Hiking in India.

Pakistani border, a task that required long hours of flying made more difficult by the lack of qualified staff. He was required to both fly and navigate the aircraft and at the same time keep the Hindu and Muslim officials, who were obliged to accompany him, from killing one another.

Des left the RAF after ten years service and joined the Hindusthan Aircraft Company as sales manager in Calcutta. This company was principally engaged in importing American light aircraft such as the Ryan Navian, Luscombe Silvaire, Aeronca Sedan and Republic Seabee Amphibians. The Seabee had been imported by Sinclair Murray & Co, a Calcutta jute firm with major interests in East Bengal, West Bengal and Orissa. Desmond was asked to fly the first of the amphibious aircraft to arrive, until such time as a qualified pilot could be engaged and brought out to India. His brother Gillian was contacted in the UK. He had been trained by the US Navy on Flying Boats at

Pensacola during the War and was offered the job on completion of certain formalities.

The Seabee had a dubious reputation as being underpowered which made them at times dangerous in inexperienced hands. The day after his brother arrived in Calcutta Desmond carried out an air test with Douglas Keiller, a Director in Sinclair Murray. Owing to a faulty fuel gauge they ran out of fuel when directly over the city but safely force-landed on the Maidan, Calcutta's Central Park close to the Victoria Memorial. It caused a great stir and a large crowd gathered. The next day he flew back to Dum Dum taking off from the 'Red Road' which had been used as a fighter airstrip during the Second World War.

Des handed over to his younger brother Gillian, who had now joined Sinclair Murray, and went off to find more enjoyable flying. For a while he went back to his old job of flying instructor and joined the Bengal Flying Club at Barrackpore as CFI (Chief Flying Instructor). He enjoyed this kind of work and did many hours teaching young pupils their initial flying before moving on to become airline pilots with the Indian Airlines Corporation and Air India.

A tragic incident occurred shortly after he took up this appointment. When returning to the airfield from a flight with a pupil he was told that his friend Hem Choudhry had crashed into the river Hooghly while instructing an American pupil. Des rushed over to find both their wives standing distraught on the bank and no sign of the plane. They had been doing spinning exercises in a DeHavilland Chipmunk and had failed to recover from a spin. Subsequent to similar accidents a modification was made in the design of the aircraft to make it safer.

Desmond immediately stripped off and with a long rope plunged into the muddy Hooghly river. After several attempts he located the plane at a depth of about sixteen feet and with the assistance of onlookers on the bank, friends and local Indians he

Louis Mountbatten 1946. RAF Mauripur Base.

secured the rope around the tail and they dragged the plane out. Both pilots were dead.

In 1949 he resigned as CFI at the Flying Club and started his career as a survey pilot with the Indian Air Survey Company at Dum Dum by Calcutta International Airport. He was now working full time on aero-survey, flying DeHavilland Rapides, mostly in India.

At this time he was involved in an air rescue operation. On Boxing day 1949 his brother Gillian and a friend decided to have a day at the beach at Digah. On the way past Desmond's house at Dum Dum they collected his seven year old daughter Maureen, and took her along for the ride. They intended to join other Flying Club members who normally went to the beach at Digah but instead they decided to go on to Dalhousie Island.

On arrival over the island there were no other planes on the beach so his brother decided to fly to a beach on nearby Halliday

With Sir Archibald Nye, High Commissioner India,
13th October 1950. Bamrauli Aerodrome.

Island. He landed on the sand just above the water's edge and while taxiing up the beach the propeller of the Sentinel L5 clipped a half buried log. On inspection the chip seemed minor so he decided to return to Calcutta in case any further problems arose. He took off and was just airborne when a section of the prop flew off with a tremendous vibration. Immediately cutting power, he put the aircraft back on the beach and they all leapt out. Luckily there was no fire although there was a strong smell of fuel due to a split in the starboard fuel tank.

They spent the remaining hours of daylight collecting driftwood for a fire, not only for warmth but to discourage the attentions of tigers which were in this uninhabited area of the Sunderbunds. On returning from their foraging for firewood the adults found young Maureen had finished off the remains of the picnic including some dregs of beer. She had scoffed the

Catching butterflies in Thailand, 1952.

lot leaving them with no drinking water or food. They spent an uncomfortable night on the beach in the vicinity of a herd of wild pigs. Fortunately the next day, after a search which lasted many hours, Des found them and after the prop was repaired they all got safely out.

Early in 1951 Desmond was transferred to the main base of Fairey Airsurveys at White Waltham. He remained with them until 1957 when he joined the Hunting Survey Company in Johannesburg as operations manager.

His new career as survey pilot was to take him through India, Pakistan and east to Thailand. One product of his travels to far off and exotic places was his interest in butterflies. He became a keen collector, eventually putting together a comprehensive collection. One of his contracts took him to the forest areas of Thailand and every spare moment when not in the air he would be hiking cross country, butterfly net in hand. Here, too, he saw the great Indian elephants at work on the construction of roads and other projects. For a while he forgot the war and his life was full as he explored, mapped, visited ancient places and got to know India, Thailand and other neighbouring nations.

As a survey pilot Des visited some extraordinary places where he came into contact with many interesting people: officials, pilots, high commissioners and dignitaries. He was highly respected as one of the best survey pilots available and he perfected his own specialised techniques to cope with the special demands of the job. At one stage he was contracted to do a survey of a proposed road into Tibet. This was dangerous work and required superb flying skills and he flew over spectacular areas of the Himalayan Mountains. These mountains were so high that often Des had to push the aircraft to its limits and found himself skimming the ridges at a few hundred feet. The opportunity to see the grandeur of the mountains towering above him and the deep valleys far below was reward enough.

Africa

After joining Hunting Air Surveys his flying took him all over the Persian Gulf, north to the Caspian Sea and eventually to Africa where he flew in southern and central Africa, north Africa, Ethiopia, Uganda, Nigeria, Ghana, Kenya, Tanzania, Malawi, South West Africa (Namibia), Angola, Northern and Southern Rhodesia (Zambia and Zimbabwe), Bechuanaland (Botswana), Mozambique and South Africa. Over the years he visited many wild areas and isolated communities. Because he covered so many miles he saw many rare sights and remote areas seldom seen before. In Ethiopia he flew through a swarm of locusts that completely blackened his windscreen. Unable to see he opened a side window and landed the plane on a rough bush strip to escape the swarm. Covering vast areas from the Middle East to

India and to Africa he spent long months away from home and the family was often apart for too long. This was to have sad repercussions later.

Reunion

Des first visited Rhodesia (now Zimbabwe) in 1951 on a survey mission with Fairey Air Surveys. He returned on several occasions. In 1957 he and the family left Britain and set up base in Johannesburg with the Hunting Air Survey Company where he worked on contracts for the British Overseas Survey Dept. Something wonderful happened on the night before he left Britain. Once again there seemed to be a divine plan in the timing.

His family was away on this final night saying farewell to relatives and the following day they were due to catch the *Cape Town Castle* at Southampton. Des went down to the pub for a

Des and Ivo Tonder. Reunion 1994.

final drink and met a fellow who gave him his business card. Des read it with excitement. It said Tonder Arts Ltd. On enquiry it turned out to be Ivo Tonder's company. After the war Ivo had left Czechoslovakia because the communists had taken over. He settled in Britain and started an art business. He was due to return that very night from a trip to London. With great excitement Des and his friend went down to the station and sure enough Ivo stepped off the last train from London. He greeted Des with the familiar 'Plunk, Plunk' just as he had so many years ago in Gestapo custody. What a thrill for the two men to be reunited after so long!

There was no sleep that night and they talked until sunrise recalling the trials and sufferings of the war, but mostly the good times. How strange it is that often the bad memories are forgotten, Des thought. He recalled all the loyal friends he had made and how adversity had welded them together. He remembered how he owed his life to so many, to Freddie who had helped him overcome the Nazis and to Honso who shared his food, to the British officers who made sure he recovered in camp hospital and to many others who risked their own lives to help him. Freddie had settled in Czechoslovakia after the war and Des and Ivo exchanged news about him. Now Ivo and Des were reunited and the kindred spirits of friends who had faced death together were rekindled in lasting ties of devotion. Next morning Des went off to Africa a happy man.

He was to have many happy hours flying in Africa. One unforgettable time was in 1962 when he flew over Mount Kilimanjaro and dropped three paratroopers on its summit. This set the world record for the highest parachute jump and landing. At the time he was based at Moshi and was asked to pilot the craft for the jump. Des had taken a full course in 'para' drops while in India so was well qualified for the attempt. Mount Kilimanjaro stands at 5,895 metres and is often covered in cloud.

For the attempt to be successful Des would have to take off early and hope for a clear day. Three French military paratroopers were to attempt the jump and they were supported by a ground team that had to climb the mountain and be ready to receive them. They loaded up and took off. After gaining height Des circled the summit only to find that the ground party had not yet reached the intended drop zone. They returned to base and several hours later took off for another attempt. Thick cloud covered the mountain but fortunately the summit was above the clouds. The view of the mountain peak standing majestically through the sea of white was breathtaking. The three para-troopers jumped and one landed within ten yards of the target.

It was in 1965 that he and the family moved to Rhodesia (now Zimbabwe) where many ex RAF personnel also lived. Des renewed friendships. He continued to fly on air surveys for various development schemes. He was commissioned to do an extensive air survey of Namibia and flew over most of the barren vastness and rugged hills of this desert area photo-graphing the terrain. On another occasion he was employed by a company doing aerial surveys in Mozambique. The war for independence in that country was heating up and Des found himself once more operating under war conditions. Flak burst around his plane and his mind suddenly took him back to the war days. With consternation he realised the urgency of the situation. He was in a civilian plane miles from anywhere and the guerilla armies had anti-aircraft guns and heat seeking missiles. There was no time to lose. They high-tailed it out of the danger zone as fast as they could.

The Crash

In Rhodesia Des met up with many ex Air Force men and ex POWs. He began to spend more and more time in bars, reminiscing about the war days. He had many friends but

Des's first accident. Salisbury Airport, 10th December 1971.

somehow Des was restless and never seemed to be at real peace. During his long flying career Des had several exciting experiences but only one serious accident. On 10th December 1971 he crashed at Salisbury (now Harare) airport in a D.H. Dove aircraft. He was instructing a young Canadian and had 'feathered' one engine a number of times; the battery had been worn down resulting in power loss to the propeller pitch control mechanism. As he approached the runway he was unable to unfeather it and Des could not get the situation under control. The plane undershot the runway, broke the under-carriage, came down on its belly, screeched to a halt and immediately caught fire. As they scrambled out Des looked back on yet another close call and the first real accident of his long flying career. He admits that at the time he was in a disturbed state of mind – his marriage had just broken up. This was more than a crash – Des's whole life was crumbling around him.

CHAPTER 8

Another Prison – Another Escape

'How shall we escape if we neglect so great salvation?'

All his life Des had carried with him an assurance in God but it had not always been foremost in his thoughts. As a youngster Des had grown up in the Christian faith. His Presbyterian grandparents had lived by the 'Book' and later at Rossall School Des had been confirmed in the Anglican Church. He recalls the day of his confirmation under Bishop Blunt. As the Bishop laid his hands on Des's head and prayed for him, Des knew that something had happened which he could not explain. Des attended a youth camp in the hills of Wales where the truth of the Gospel found a lasting place in his heart. He came under the instruction of deep, committed teachers who spoke at length with him about God and Christ. As a young lad he committed his life to Christ; his faith never left him and gave him strength through the difficulties he endured. Des was aware of some higher power looking after him and helping him in times of trouble.

After the hardships of war he embarked on his successful and highly varied career and Des felt no need to pursue spiritual things. He had a loving wife and expanding family; after Maureen had come Michael and Joan. Des and his family enjoyed good times together in exciting and adventurous places all around the world. Suddenly all this was over. He had just crashed a highly expensive aircraft and his home was in tatters.

For years Des had been hounded by guilt and an increasing sense of emptiness and failure. After the war he suffered with ulcers and although they healed his spiritual condition remained scarred. Always with him, the sense of guilt and rejection had affected his personality and he had become imprisoned by his own war experiences. He had taken to drink and was absorbed by his flying activities. As a husband and father he had given his family no spiritual guidance and a great vacuum existed. Des had simply filled his own life more and more with his career. One day he came home to find his wife had filled the vacuum – not with another man but by joining the Jehovah's Witnesses. Des was confused. He could not understand why she had done so. Had they not always been Christians and belonged to a church? Had he not always believed in Christ? But for his wife the situation had become untenable and much to Des's consternation she felt she could no longer go on. His upbringing and grounding in the faith prevented Des from joining the sect and the two parted. Des sank into a new era of darkness and confusion. He did not know what to do. Where could he go to find help? Alone and hurt, for the first time in many years he began to seek the Lord. He turned to the faith of his childhood and began to pray and to read the Bible, seeking answers! He thought that if he could just find enough scriptures he would be able to prove that the sect was wrong. Instead he was convicted of his own need to come back to God.

The Amazing Events of his Past
As Des's faith renewed he realised more and more the incredible deliverance that God had wrought in his life. Thinking back on past events he recalled how he had survived the war: being shot down and captured, the prison life, the Kugel Order given by Hitler himself the Gestapo incarceration, solitary

confinement, the starvation diet, and many other dangers. He knew that someone bigger than him had watched over him. He remembered the nightmare of rejection by his own people and his near suicide, and the voice that prevented him from taking his own life. He saw the hand of God in these events. He thought about the life, death and resurrection of Christ, how Christ had been so cruelly treated and falsely accused, rejected by his own, imprisoned, tortured and killed, and on the third day risen again. He remembered the beckoning light of the church in Domazlitze bidding him to draw near to God. And he remembered Easter 1944 when he had entered the Gestapo hell believing his days were numbered. Only God could have saved him, he concluded.

Recalling the faith of his grandparents and his youthful commitment to the Lord as a teenager, Des decided to recommit his life to Christ. Immediately the heavy guilt that had become so much part of him over the years lifted and he began to live again as a free man. For many years he had been a prisoner; now he was beginning to experience the spiritual release and healing which he needed so much. Like other people Des had suffered deep heartaches: he had lost a child at birth and two of his dear grandchildren had been tragically killed in a freak accident. Now his family had split. Not only that but for years he had become imprisoned by a life of selfishness. The scars of war and the unseen bonds that had entangled around him had distorted his personality and held him prisoner. They began to fall away and he started to rebuild a shattered life. For so long he had sought freedom in flying – to get away from it all, up in the boundless skies where earthly restrictions were no longer present and where he could forget the past and his own failures. There he had found release and the sense of God's presence. This had been Des's way of coping. Up there heaven seemed nearer. But he always had to come down to earth. Now he was free of the guilt that had driven him and he could start living again. At last he was coming to understand the love of God.

'For I am convinced that nothing can ever separate us from His love. Death can't, and life can't. The angels won't, and all the powers of hell itself cannot keep God's love away. Our fears for today, our worries about tomorrow, or where we are - high above the sky, or in the the deepest ocean - nothing will ever be able to separate us from the love of God demonstrated by our Lord Jesus Christ when he died for us.' (Living Bible, Romans 8:38,39.)

The Man Himself
Des retired from flying in 1975 but continued to assist as a navigator for a local survey company for many years. As he became less active in his flying career Des took to keeping bees. In order to get around his widely distributed hives he used a small motorbike and he became a familiar figure scooting from place to place. To transport his bees he had an old Morris van which could quite often be seen stacked high with hives and followed by swarms of furious bees. African bees are well known for their ferocious nature and Des would appear dressed to the hilt in all his gear, laughing his head off at how many had stung him.

Des had many contacts with alcoholics and a special compassion for those who were down and out. At any one time there were numerous homeless men sharing his digs. He would feed them and share the gospel with them.

His approach to life is one of extreme optimism, thankfulness and contentment. He has great joy in testifying to all he meets about the abounding goodness of God. His approach to his faith may be thought by some to be quite eccentric for he spares no opportunity to speak about the salvation of God through Christ.

Driving 1936 MG.

He delights to tell others of the great things God has done for him and the faithfulness of God in answered prayers. He constantly reminds others of God's promise of eternal life through His Son Jesus Christ. But he is totally non-denominational or sectarian in his approach and mixes freely with Christians of different persuasions. He simply proclaims the Lordship of Jesus and the need for all to come to a personal trust and faith in Christ as Saviour. His all-consuming wish is that as many people as possible should have a personal faith in Christ as Lord.

Typical of this fearless witness was an occasion when he visited Jerusalem on a group tour. The group booked in at a local hospice and were given very strict instructions that they should be back no later than 11 pm as the doors were locked each night and not opened until dawn the following day. Des went off on his own and enjoyed himself so much that he forgot the time. When he did arrive back at the hospice the heavy doors were bolted and no one around. Des was locked out. Without another thought Des went off to the nearest police station where he told those on duty about the soon coming Messiah and requested a bed for the night

He speaks highly of his family and with evident joy at the grandchildren God has given him. When he attended the marriage of his granddaughter he gleefully informed her that he was anticipating at least three great-grandchildren. He is generous and gives sacrificially without others knowing. He is never happier than when serving his Lord. Fearless in his witness, joyful in his daily life and content in his circumstances, he is a living witness to the incredible goodness of God who delivered him from the gates of hell, extended his life and gave it meaning. He is indeed a witness to the greatest escape of all – from sin and death into the salvation of God through His Son, Jesus Christ.

The Survivors

Many prisoners died during the Second World War. Six million Jews and at least another six million other nationalities, Poles, Czechs, Dutch, French, Germans and others, including Jehovah's Witnesses, Seventh Day Adventists, Pentecostals, Catholics, Protestants and Orthodox died in prisons and concentration camps, not to mention the millions of other casualties. Yet there were survivors – from every walk of life. The Biblical prophet Isaiah states that God will always have a witness.

'You are my witnesses, declares the Lord, and I am God.'
Isaiah 43:12

They are the witnesses of the things that happened, lest the world should forget or deny it. Des was one – witness to war and hardship, to prison and escape, to brave men who perished.

Through history it seems that in the midst of conflict, tragedy and trial some survive. Des was chosen to be such a one. He is a voice for thousands of POWs who suffered the traumas of imprisonment and looked into the stark face of death. He is witness to the events of the Great Escape and to those that participated in it. He is also witness to the reality of the Christian faith. He witnesses not only to God's keeping power but also to a future hope that loved ones will be reunited, that suffering and injustice will end, that broken lives will one day be healed and broken homes united.

The life of Desmond Plunkett bears witness that even in the face of overwhelming evil and despair, human weakness and failure, faith and goodness triumphs through the love of God.

Of the seventy six men who escaped that fateful night of 24th March 1944 only twenty six survived. After the war the British RAF Special Investigation Branch brought to trial many of those Nazis who committed the murders. Twenty one Gestapo personnel who were directly involved with the murder of the airmen were found guilty of war crimes and executed. Eleven committed suicide and seventeen were imprisoned for varying lengths of time. But Des bears no malice: when he recommitted his life to God he made a point of forgiving in prayer all those who had ill treated him. 1994 was the fiftieth anniversary of the Great Escape and Des says he is ready to go on to the new millennium. When his captors told him he only had a few days to live and held him under threat of imminent execution, they had not taken into account the hand of God. His life was extended for more than half a century and he continues to live one day at a time, celebrating the Greatest Escape of all – to know the love of God through Jesus Christ

If one day you are stopped by a wizened little man with a twinkle in his eyes and a laugh in his spirit, who tells you about the love of God – do not belittle him, it could be Des.

Desmond Plunkett now resides in an RAF Association Nursing Home in the United Kingdom.

Des echoes the Psalmist:

'This will be written for the generation to come; that a people yet to be created may praise the Lord. For He looked down from His holy height; from heaven the Lord gazed upon the earth, to hear the groaning of the prisoner; to set free those who were doomed to death; that men may tell of the name of the Lord.'

Psalm 102:18.

Interview with Desmond Plunkett

Question: 'You escaped almost certain death on a number of occasions. Thinking back in retrospect, why do you think you survived such incredible odds?'

Des: 'I believe the prayers of my grandparents and parents protected me through life. They were very devout and my grandfather grounded me in the faith with the many Bible stories he told me. This helped me through. My father too was a Christian and my mother certainly was. Their prayers made the difference for me.'

Question: 'What is the most significant thing for you in it all?'

With tears in his eyes Des replies: 'The wonderful assurance of God's forgiveness. To know that I am accepted by God is the most amazing thing of all.'

His story declares that God cares. God is still able to help in the most difficult times, when all human resources are gone and when you stand alone. Reach out to Him.

Let Us Salute Them

On Friday 25th March 1994 a memorial service attended by many hundreds was held at St Clement's Danes, London, the

Central Church of the Royal Air Force. The resident chaplain read the following dedication:

'As we remember those who, fifty years ago, lost their lives during Operation Escape 200, post-war named the Great Escape, from Stalag Luft 3, Sagan, Germany, in March and April 1944, LET US SALUTE THEM and all those members of the Royal Air Force, Dominion and Allied Air Forces who died in the service of their Country. We pledge to keep alive the memory of those who died for the cause of justice, freedom and peace. Reverently and gratefully, we will remember them.

Dame Vera Lynn, DBE, LLD, MMus, the forces' sweetheart, gave a rendering of 'We'll Meet Again'.

At the end of the service the Blessing was pronounced:

Go forth into the world in peace; be of good courage; hold fast that which is good; render to no man evil for evil. Strengthen the faint hearted, support the weak; help the afflicted; honour all men. Love and serve the Lord, rejoicing in the power of the Holy Spirit. And the blessing of God Almighty, the Father, the Son, and the Holy Spirit be with you all this day and evermore.

Bibliography

Paul Brickhill, *The Great Escape* (Faber and Faber Ltd., London).
Allan Burgess, *The Longest Tunnel* (Grove Weidenfeld, New York).
Lord Russell, *The Scourge of the Swastika* (Cassell & Co. Ltd., London).
William Shirer, *The Rise and Fall of the Third Reich* (Secker and Warburg, London).
Eric Williams, *The Wooden Horse* (Collins, London).

Biblical References

p. 9   Isaiah 40 v.31
p. 12   Psalm 23 v.4
p. 28   Psalm 142 v.6
p. 43   Psalm 27 v.5
p. 56   Job 38 v.17
p. 76   Psalm 102 vv. 19, 20
p. 88   Revelation 21 v.5
p. 100 Hebrews 2 v.3